PARIS STREET STYLE
SHOES

BY ISABELLE THOMAS & FRÉDÉRIQUE VEYSSET

UNDER THE DIRECTION OF CAROLINE LEVESQUE

ILLUSTRATIONS BY CLÉMENT DEZELUS
PHOTOGRAPHS BY FRÉDÉRIQUE VEYSSET

ABRAMS IM▲GE
NEW YORK

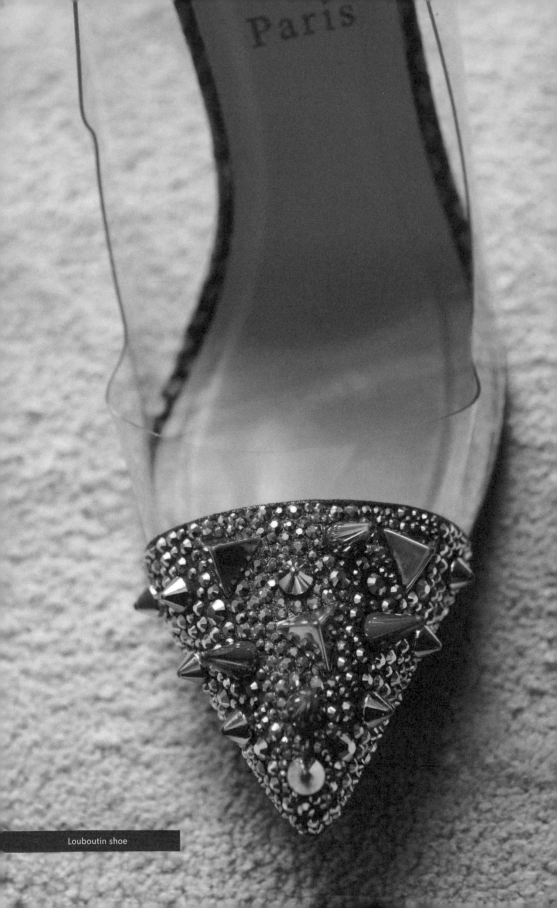
Louboutin shoe

CONTENTS

. . . .

"*You weren't made on an assembly line, so be unique.*"

Manolo Blahnik

AREN'T WE ALL CRAZY ABOUT SHOES?

. . . .

More than our shade of lipstick or the length of our hemline, our shoes reveal how we feel on any given day. Body-armor boots, all-terrain running shoes, killer pumps, or, our current heartthrob, oxfords—they reflect our state of mind and our many lives even as they determine the image we want to project.

We may not all be shoe addicts—*oh, really?*—but our eyes still sparkle at the sight of a new pair of shoes. After all, what could be more intimate than the gift of a pair of stiletto heels from the man you love? Look how he sees me! As a princess? A goddess? Perched on high heels, we own our ability to be fragile and strong at the same time. And it doesn't matter if we hardly ever wear heels, we like having them anyway.

Even in hard times we stay true to our passion. Our grocery bags may get lighter, but we don't deny ourselves shoes. Whether amateur collectors or passionate professionals, we know that shoes have the power to give new life to our wardrobe and transform our appearance with a click of the heels.

Looking at beautiful shoes, we can lose our grip on reality. If there is a woman out there who hasn't convinced herself that four-inch spikes will, with a little training, become as comfortable as slippers, or that "one size too small" is just an insignificant detail compared to the gorgeous line of the coveted shoe, let her throw the first pair of leopard-print slingbacks!

Clothing stores have caught on and started interspersing their merchandise with enticing sandals, sneakers, pumps, and ballet flats. And online sales of shoes have shot through the roof. People are less and less afraid of buying a pair without trying them on first. Click, another pair purchased!

How about you? What will you choose for your next pair of shoes?

"The lower I feel, the higher the heel."

Giovanna Battaglia, fashion writer

"Jeans should give you a great butt, and shoes should give you great feet."

Annabel Winship, shoe designer

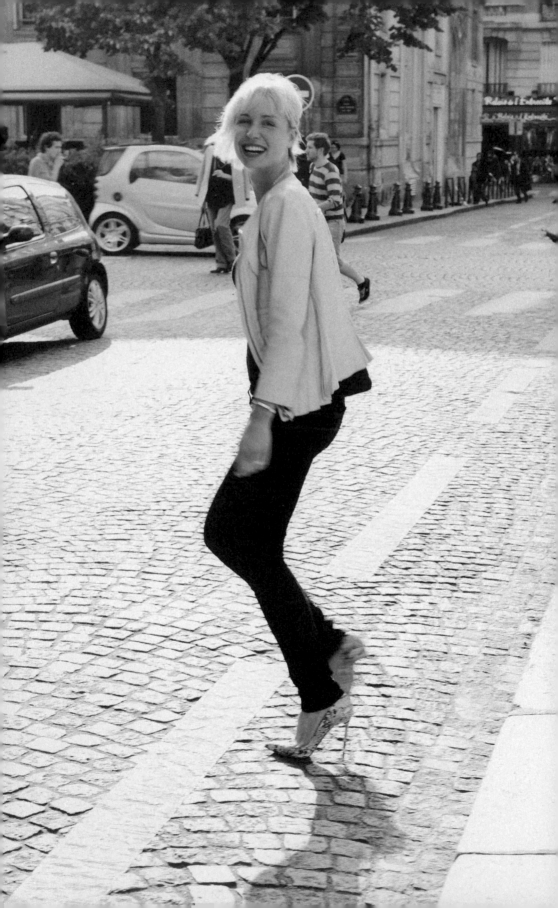

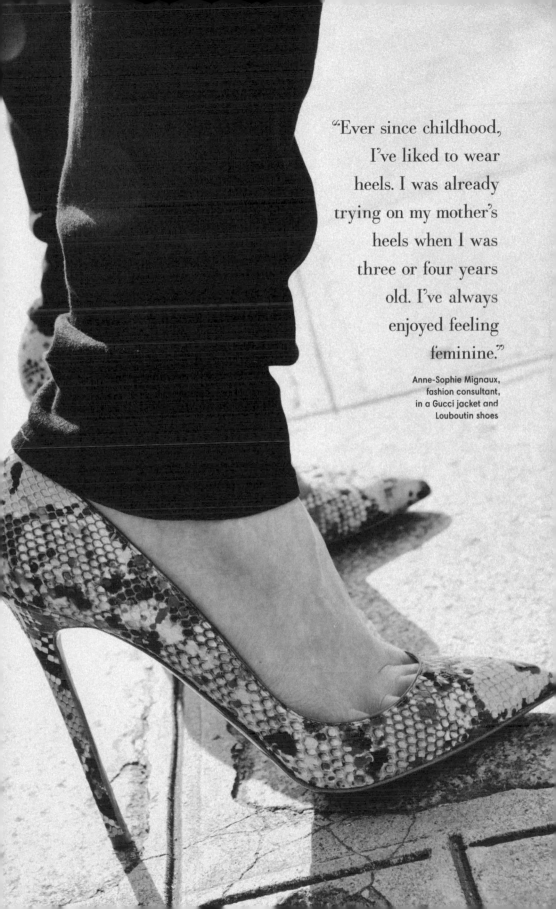

"Ever since childhood, I've liked to wear heels. I was already trying on my mother's heels when I was three or four years old. I've always enjoyed feeling feminine."

Anne-Sophie Mignaux, fashion consultant, in a Gucci jacket and Louboutin shoes

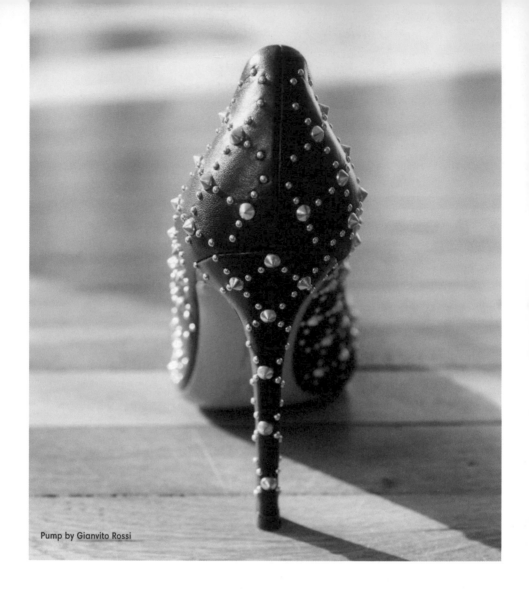

Pump by Gianvito Rossi

GET A LITTLE
ALTITUDE

Starting about ten years ago, super-high heels started to appear on runways and in the streets. They can be five, six, even seven inches high with raised soles or platforms. Beware of having the ungainly gait of a stork; the highest heels are not for every build!

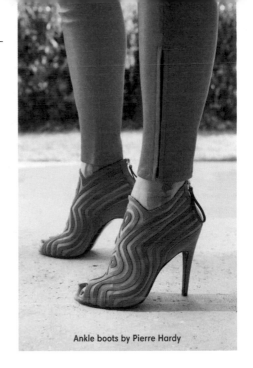

Ankle boots by Pierre Hardy

Heels existed in ancient Greece and Rome, but it was the self-consciously short Catherine de Médicis who revived the fashion in the fourteenth century. Wanting to be visible at a distance, the future queen of France drew her inspiration from Venetian chopines, which were platform shoes reaching up to twenty-eight inches in height that were designed to protect women from the mud and filth in the street. "A third part wood, a third part adornment, and a third part woman," as they said of Catherine at the time. When she married Henry II of France, she brought the wooden heels in her baggage, and very soon French men and women started wearing them too. The demimonde quickly copied this aristocratic fashion, and prostitutes appeared on wooden heels three to four inches high. The taller the heel, the nobler and more "beyond price" a woman was.

Our modern fascination with heels, however, likely comes from Louis XIV, who wore them regularly to make himself taller. The king's flamboyant brother, known as Monsieur, started the fashion for red heels when he returned from a night at the Paris Market carnival with his shoes speckled with blood. All of the nobles, soon followed by the women of ill repute, jumped on the bandwagon.

The French Revolution put a temporary stop to this passion for height. A good revolutionary should have his feet flat on the ground, and in sober shoes! There was no question of following the decadent fashions of the brainless aristocracy, who would soon enough be headless!

Heels made a quiet comeback at the end of the nineteenth century, but this time only women wore them. They stayed modest in height until advances in technology allowed shoemakers to lengthen them, strengthen them, and make them bolder. In the 1920s, the designer Charles Jourdan had the idea of slenderizing the heel—which was first made of wood or plastic—and giving it extra height. Then, in 1954, Roger Vivier, working for Christian Dior, experimented with reinforcing the heel with a metal rod, allowing him to make it even more slender while remaining sturdy. After that, there were no practical limits to a heel's height. Hollywood stars from Marilyn Monroe to Ava Gardner wore them, amping up their sex appeal with their swaying

> *"I don't know who invented high heels, but all women owe him a lot!"*
> MARILYN MONROE

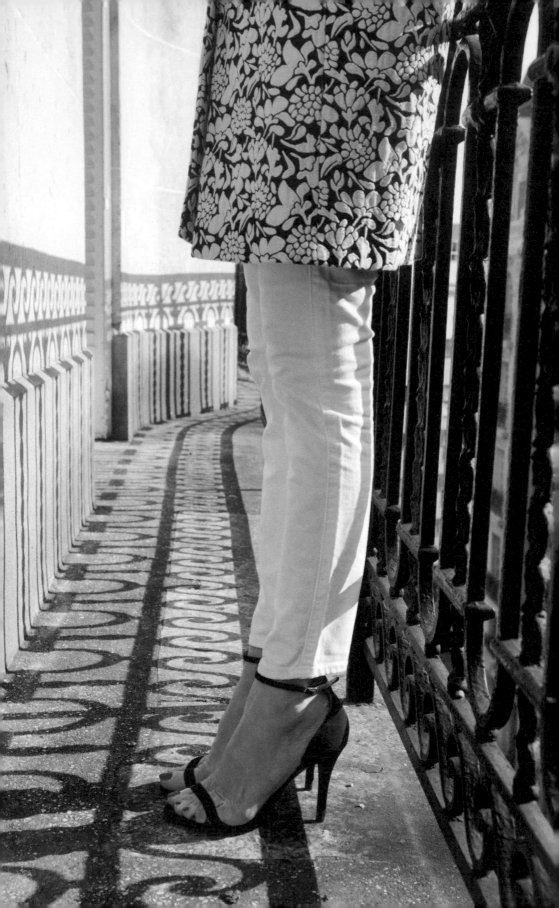

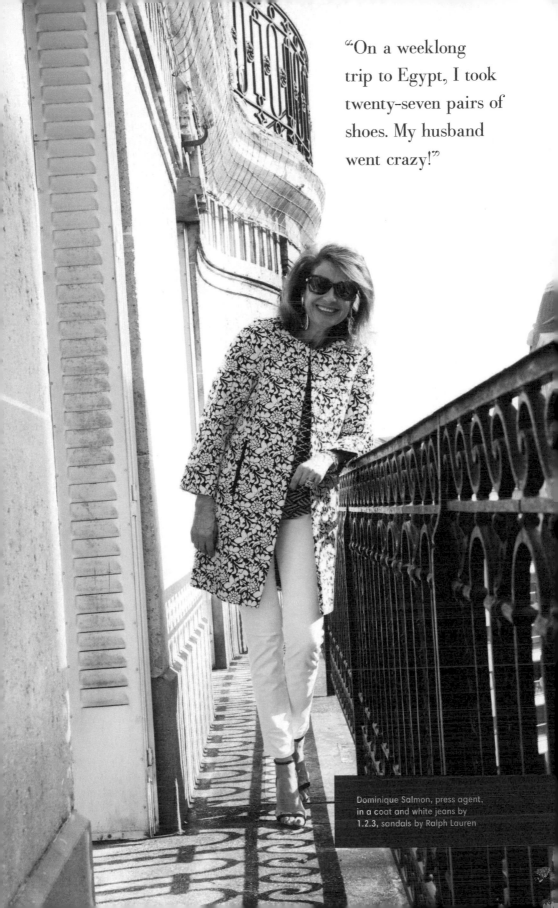

"On a weeklong trip to Egypt, I took twenty-seven pairs of shoes. My husband went crazy!"

Dominique Salmon, press agent, in a coat and white jeans by 1.2.3, sandals by Ralph Lauren

gait. "I don't know who invented high heels," said Marilyn, "but all women owe him a lot!"

During the 1990s, the ultra-high heel came into fashion. Tom Ford, working with Carine Roitfeld and Mario Testino, would make Gucci the warrior for porno chic and the heel his preferred weapon. The very high heel became at once sexy and rebellious. In that same period, Christian Louboutin and Manolo Blahnik would transform women into exciting cabaret dancers and striptease artists, objects of fantasy and women of power.

With these designers, the ultra-high heel became democratized, to the point where it is now widely seen as a symbol of both seduction and power. The editors at *Vogue Paris*, for instance, claim that they never step outside without their heels.

MASTERING HIGH HEELS

When people used to talk about high heels, it was to say how terrifying they found an additional three inches of height. Today that sounds like a joke! Three inches? Heel sizes have doubled. Six-inch heels are no longer just part of S and M fantasies. Ever since Victoria Beckham started appearing in spike-heeled stilettos, they have popped up in every store window. Our eyes are getting used to these crazy heights. But what about our feet?

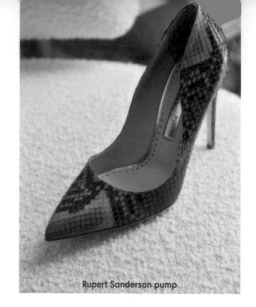

Rupert Sanderson pump

SOME CAN'T LIVE WITHOUT THEIR HEELS

In flats some women feel too small, and they can't bear to crane their necks to talk to someone taller, especially when negotiating an important business contract. Others say that wearing flats makes them feel heavy. Arletty, the French actress, believed that women should always wear heels: "It raises your fanny," she said in her Parisian drawl.

And some can't come back down: After an extended time on stilts, their calf muscles retract. They get cramps in their calves and aches in their backs as soon as they try on a pair of loafers or ballerinas. They need to wear at least four-inch heels in order to feel comfortable.

. . . .

"When a pair of shoes hurts, you have to stop wearing them. They can injure your feet and the damage can unfortunately be permanent."

Nathalie Elharrar, creator of the LaRare line

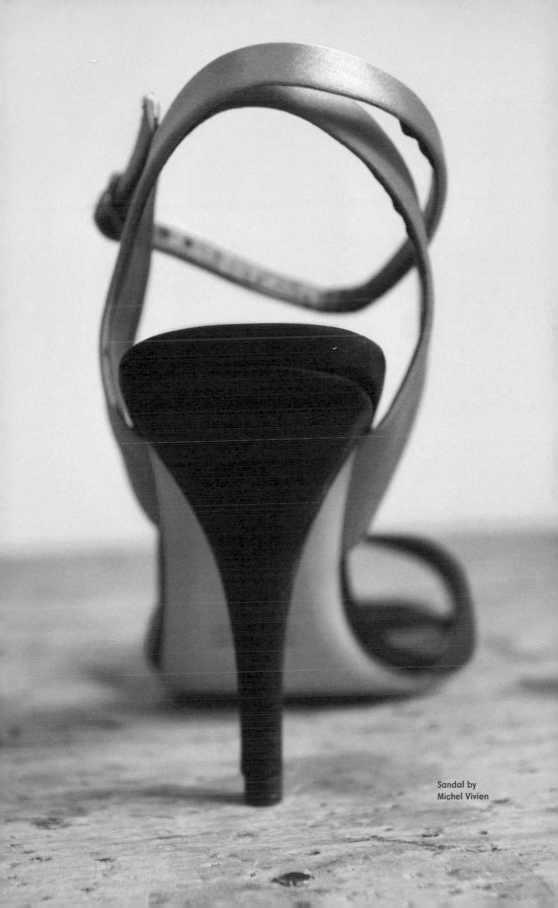

Sandal by
Michel Vivien

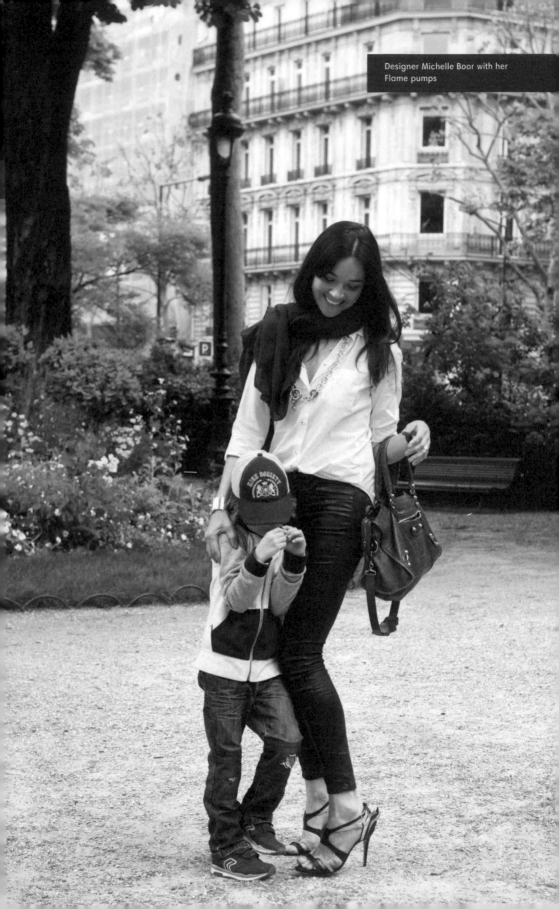

Designer Michelle Boor with her Flame pumps

It's true: Heels look good on a woman...if she wears them well. You sometimes come across women walking like wobbly herons or swaggering like truckers on six-inch heels. Yikes.

Is wearing high heels an innate skill? Yes, for some but it can also be learned. There are even schools to teach you how!

But just follow these seven rules and you can skip class:

RULE NUMBER ONE
Find Heels That Are Right for You

Your office mate may find her sandals perfectly comfortable, but it doesn't mean that you will thrive in her shoes. The shape of your foot may be entirely different. The only solution is to try on many different models (and not necessarily the most expensive brands). Your arch needs to be held in firm contact with the bottom of the shoe, which should marry the curve of your foot. The heel has to work for you; that's all. Every brand uses a different last (the model around which a shoe is shaped during manufacture); it's up to you to find the one that fits best.

RULE NUMBER TWO
Know Your Shoe Size

It seems obvious. Except that sometimes you fall between two sizes. With heels, it's important to get your shoe size exactly right. Too wide a footbed and your foot will not be supported (with loafers or flat-heeled boots, it matters less). If the salesgirl says, "They'll adapt to your foot," because she doesn't have your size, don't believe her. True, leather stretches a little, but it will never stretch a whole size. Silk, fabric, and patent leather don't stretch at all!

RULE NUMBER THREE
Don't Focus on the Height

A medium-high heel can be more uncomfortable than a very high one if the arch of the shoe (the angle between the heel and the forefoot) is too severe. If the angle is too sharp, all your

THE 10 COMMANDMENTS FOR WALKING WELL IN HEELS

1. Set your heel down first, as you would in flat shoes.

2. Walk up and down stairs slowly as many times as you need to until you feel confident.

3. Avoid cobblestones.

4. Stand straight, with your shoulders back and your head high.

5. Take your time. You can't walk at the same pace in heels as you can in flats.

6. Keep a reasonable distance between your feet, placing them neither in a straight line nor like parallel railroad tracks.

7. Look straight ahead, not at your feet.

8. Put your hips in motion; give them their freedom to move.

9. Re-watch *Niagara* by Henry Hathaway, if only to admire the swaying walk of the young Marilyn Monroe.

10. Have confidence in yourself.

weight rests on the ball of your foot. If the curve is right, your foot sits comfortably, your body takes naturally to being vertical, and you can trot around all day on five-inch heels.

———— **RULE NUMBER FOUR** ————
Change the Way You Walk

You can't walk in heels the way you do in flats. Your steps have to be shorter and your gait slower. Your upper body needs to stay mobile; otherwise you'll look like a soldier marching at attention! If the difference isn't clear to you instinctively, then you need to practice. Imagine a straight line and follow it. Be careful on staircases (walking down them is always harder).

———— **RULE NUMBER FIVE** ————
Don't Give Up

Some women say they just can't wear heels. If they aren't interested, then they are right to forget about it. But maybe they simply haven't found the shoe that fits their particular foot. You don't give up because you bet on the wrong horse. It's worth trying again. And this time you may find the right shoemaker and the right last. If spiked heels don't work, try a pair of platform heels, which have less arch. Or wedge heels, which are often more stable.

· ·

"Even when pregnant, I love to wear high heels to modulate the curves!"

Carole Tessier

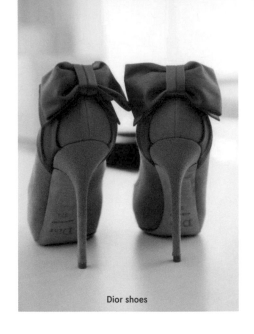
Dior shoes

———— **RULE NUMBER SIX** ————
Keep Your Toes under Control

Your toes should not be squashed inside your shoe or sticking out like unhappy prisoners when you wear open-toed shoes (remember Julianne Moore's unruly toes on the red carpet at Cannes!).

———— **RULE NUMBER SEVEN** ————
Change Shoes Often

Beware of tender spots that turn into blisters when your foot is not adequately supported. Consider changing into less drastic heels to rest your muscles and your tendons. You can wear more than one pair of shoes in a day—flats for walking, heels for the office. And the good news is that your body adapts. In high heels, the weight of your body tips forward onto the balls of your feet, and consequently, women who wear heels every day have harder, more sculpted feet. Since your whole leg is being used, you'll be delighted to know that you put on muscle just by walking around.

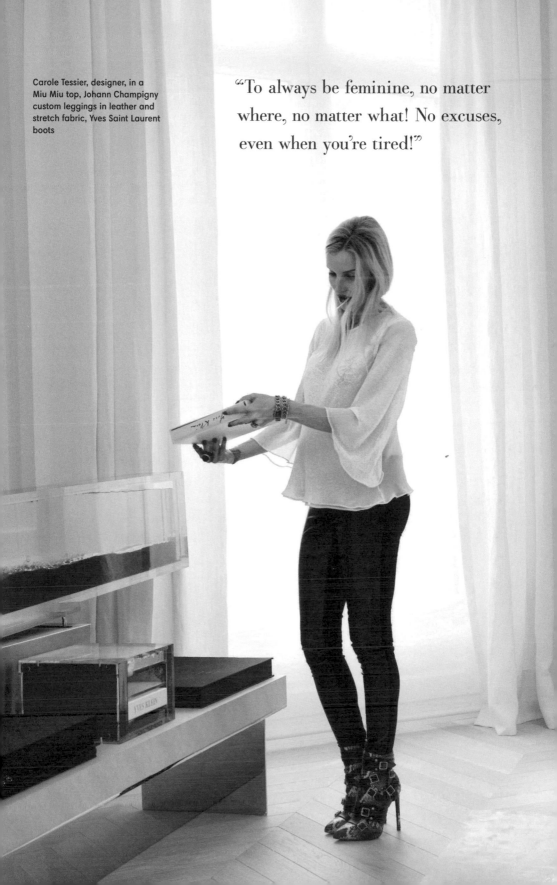

Carole Tessier, designer, in a Miu Miu top, Johann Champigny custom leggings in leather and stretch fabric, Yves Saint Laurent boots

"To always be feminine, no matter where, no matter what! No excuses, even when you're tired!"

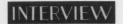

Marie-Agnès Gillot

PRINCIPAL DANCER AT THE PARIS OPERA

"Learn to move gracefully and be aware of your body, your pelvis, your back."

. . . .

Do you look at women walking in the street? How do they seem to you?

Yes, I look at them all the time, and I notice that there's often a problem. Most women walk with their legs bent and their pelvis motionless, as though it were stuck to their femurs. It lacks suppleness, fluidity. The difficulty when you're wearing heels is that your body shifts its fulcrum forward. The foot rests entirely on the ball, and to compensate for this weight shift, most women walk leaning backward.

For your walk to be pleasing, you mustn't dissociate the top from the bottom. There have to be angles; your body has to undulate. Often the toes are too bunched up. On the fashion catwalks, I'm astonished by the lack of elegance and grace on the part of some models. You can tell that they're very uncomfortable wearing heels.

Are there secrets to walking correctly in high heels?

The first thing is to develop your feet, then your legs, and to keep your knees supple. To walk attractively, the knee has to pass through the stretched position. You need to practice keeping the same progression of movements as when you walk in flats: Your heel should strike the ground first, then your hips should move, the way Naomi Campbell does so well. In heels, you need to keep your pelvis supple and flexible. It has to accompany your step. You also need to stand straight, stretch your neck, open your shoulders. Your head, which is heavy, should not be a dead weight; it's one of the first things you learn in classical dance. You "seek" upwards, you stand straight so as to put less weight on your legs.

You also need to practice walking with your feet in a line. Nothing is uglier than legs far apart and parallel. The greater the distance between your legs, the less graceful your walk.

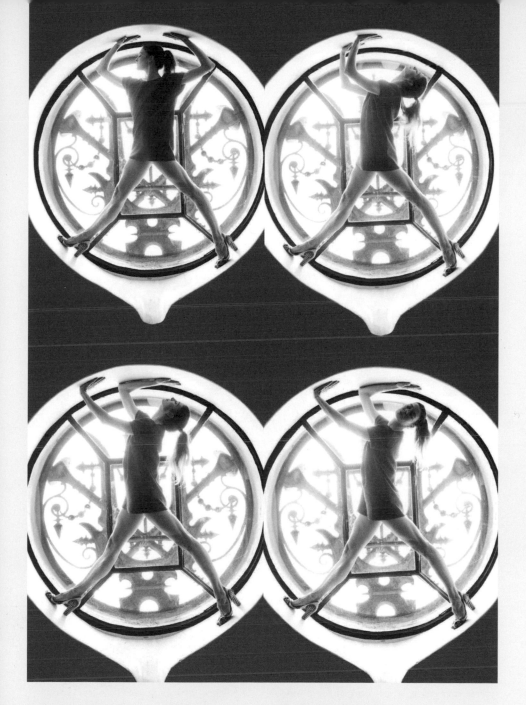

How can you go about improving your carriage?

Classical dance is good training. Even if you start late, your body adapts quickly, and the progress is rapid and visible. You learn to move gracefully and be aware of your body, your pelvis, your back.

Do you wear heels?

Yes, I wear them all the time. It rests my legs, my Achilles tendons. And it helps me relax my muscles, which are tired from standing on point and wearing ballet shoes.

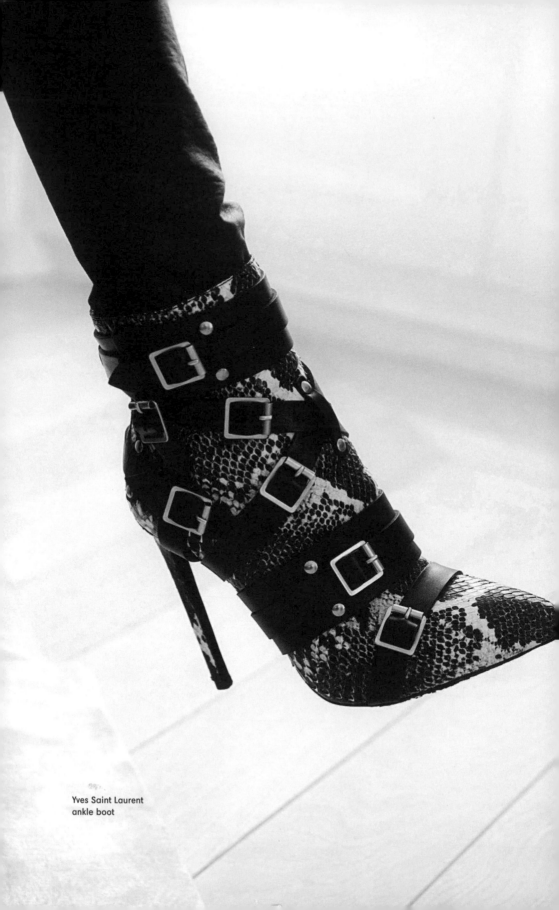

Yves Saint Laurent
ankle boot

SEX
AND THE SHOE

. . . .

For Carrie Bradshaw, there was no middle ground between super-sexy heels and going barefoot. Manolo Blahnik, Jimmy Choo, Walter Steiger, Pierre Hardy, Christian Louboutin, Dior—in episodes of Sex and the City, *our favorite shoe addict walked New York City's pavement perched on shoes made by highly coveted shoe designers. Never was a more orgasmic relation to shoes portrayed. Is Manolo sexier than Mr. Big?*

"He knelt down, kissed my shoes, kneaded them with his feverish and caressing fingers, unlaced them. And, while kissing, kneading, and caressing them, he said, in a supplicating voice, in the voice of a weeping child:

'Oh! Marie, Marie, your little shoes; give them to me directly, directly, directly. I want them directly. Give them to me.'"
—*The Diary of a Chambermaid* by Octave Mirbeau

Starting in childhood, we've been told that love will come to us with a shoe that fits our feet perfectly. The most famous shoe-fitting scene in all of literature—and in all of Disney—makes us believe that we will be transformed from Cinderella to a princess thanks to a glass slipper. In the Brothers Grimm version, the stepsisters even mutilate their feet in the hope of stuffing them into the slipper, which the psychoanalyst Bruno Bettelheim saw as a symbolic

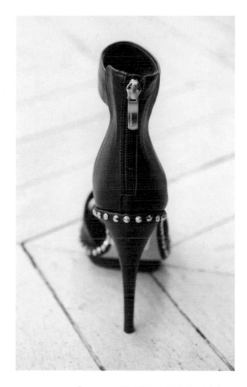

Jueconimu Bonnie pump

enactment of sexual penetration. The world's best-known fetishist was Prince Charming, who kept the lost slipper like a precious relic to guide him to the girl he loved.

"Until the nineteenth century, a woman never showed her feet outside her private chambers. Only dancers displayed them," writes Anne de Marnhac, a historian. "It was finally after World War I that hems were shortened to reveal a woman's calves and ankles." Laced ankle boots were replaced by peekaboo sandals. Flappers—with actress Louise Brooks in the lead—popularized high-heeled shoes, associated until then with disreputable women. The modern woman danced until morning, smoked, wore her hair short, ringed her eyes with eyeliner, and answered to no one!

During World War II, the pin-up girls of Gil Elvgren and Alberto Vargas sauntered into the fantasies of American GIs wearing garter belts and high heels. And Hollywood would do its part to promote the image of the sensual, seductive woman of the soldiers' dreams: the unforgettable Marilyn Monroe, Ava Gardner, Sophia Loren, Elizabeth Taylor, and Bettie Page were to become ambassadors for the stiletto heel and a conquering femininity.

ARE HIGH HEELS AN APHRODISIAC?

Lovers of "trampling," those who take pleasure in spiked heels, would say yes... and it's often just a step from spiked heels to dominance! According to research, sexual fetishism is widespread throughout the world and evenly shared by both sexes. How many women find their closets filled with stiletto heels that they will never wear on the street? What man has not offered a pair of towering heels to his mistress?

In Zhang Yimou's *Raise the Red Lantern*, there is an unforgettable scene of a ritual foot massage, which provides addictive pleasure to the woman chosen by the master. These attentions prepare her for a night of love that will give her the right to run the household for a day.

In ancient China, girls' feet were bound to keep them from growing, because tiny feet were considered a sign of aristocratic distinction. "Showing them was as immodest as uncovering one's body," writes Gérard Leleu, sexologist and author of the famous *Le traité des caresses*. "Even today, pretty feet and shoes are a symbol of hyper-femininity. Wearing heels thrusts a woman's pelvis forward, giving her a different walk. You feel the difference unconsciously.

. . . .

"I think I love [your slippers] as much as I do you."
GUSTAVE FLAUBERT WROTE TO LOUISE COLET

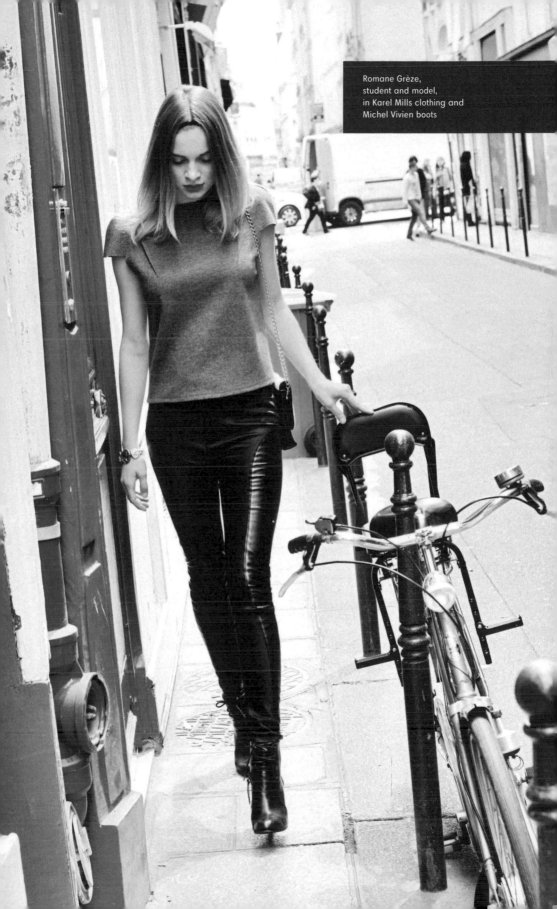

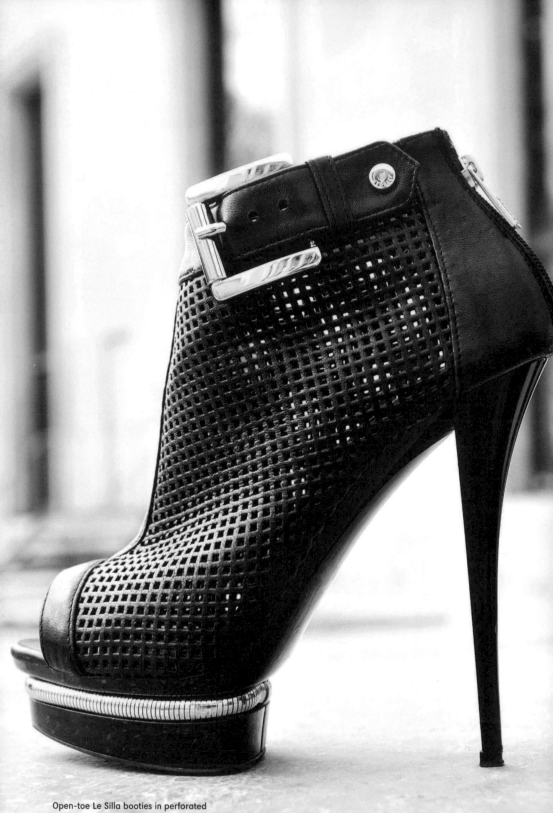

Open-toe Le Silla booties in perforated
leather with metal buckle

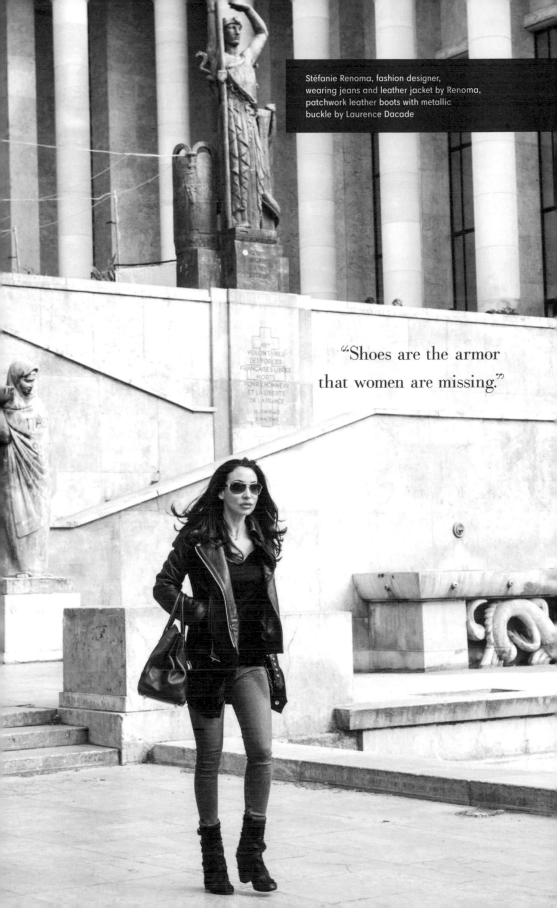

"Shoes are the armor
that women are missing."

THE TOP SEXY-SHOE MOVIES

Gentlemen Prefer Blondes
directed by Howard Hawks

The Man Who Loved Women
directed by François Truffaut

The Last Metro
directed by François Truffaut

Cinderella
produced by Walt Disney

High Heels
directed by Pedro Almodóvar

From the moment you put on beautiful shoes, you become anchored in your body, which in turn becomes more active, more present, more seductive."

"Heels are a paradox of strength and fragility," writes Isabelle Bordji, head of the Maison Ernest, which specializes in super-high heels. "In stiletto heels, you can fall at any moment; there is dominance and a need for protection. It combines the masculine and the feminine, a man's warrior side and a woman's fragility. It gives you a sort of confidence that has an effect on men. In modern society, women are no longer forced into a straightjacket; they are free to choose who they want to be. The retro movement in clothing—garter belts and very high heels—doesn't signal a regression in thinking. Men and women are equal but different, and this difference is sometimes poorly understood. Today, women wear high heels primarily for themselves: They reappropriate old codes to feel hyper-feminine."

When he was asked in a recent French edition of *Vanity Fair* what makes him handsome, Frédéric Mitterrand answered wickedly: "A pair of stiletto heels by Ernest, which specializes in oversized high heels." Both men and women covet these shoes!

According to Isabelle Bordji, "Many men buy themselves heels. They are heterosexual and often hide the fact of buying them, but sometimes they are also accompanied by their partner, and they cross-dress or just like to wear women's shoes. They like to connect with their feminine side, their emotional side. They often have positions of power and responsibility, jobs where they can't let themselves go, where they always have to be on show. It gives them a way of decompressing."

So, high heels have even become therapy, a new way to connect with one's feminine side, in a society that privileges money, success, and power.

When he was asked in a recent French edition of *Vanity Fair* what makes him handsome, Frédéric Mitterrand answered wickedly: *"A pair of stiletto heels by Ernest."*

THE MAISON ERNEST

Founded in 1904 by Ernest Amselle, the Maison Ernest has specialized in very high heels from the start. Serving an affluent clientele that has included those looking for something edgy as well as height-challenged Parisiennes, the Maison Ernest promises comfort and added height to women as well as men. Hasn't former French culture minister and journalist Frédéric Mitterrand admitted in the pages of the French *Vanity Fair* to being a fan of this Paris-based company? The Maison Ernest has profited from its long collaboration with dancers from the great cabarets, and its shoes respect the shape of the foot and support the arch. Official purveyors to everyone from Parisian caberets (e.g., the Crazy Horse, the Lido, the Folies Bergère) to Thierry Mugler's last runway show, this hundred-year-old company has also supplied such stars as Grace Jones, Bianca Jagger, and Beyoncé, not to mention Guy Bourdin and Helmut Newton. In 2012, Isabelle Bordji bought Maison Ernest and became its new director.

Christian Louboutin

SHOE DESIGNER

. . . .

Women probably say his name more often than they say the name of their own husbands, and yet the husbands aren't jealous! Louboutin, who has the brand identity of a rock star, has upheld a woman's right to be brainy even as she wears a chorus girl's shoes.

It could be said that you're the George Clooney of shoes, the favorite of the ladies. It's flattering, of course! I was brought up among women, and I'm happy to be working at a job that gives me pleasure and that gives them pleasure.

But it's beyond what I can understand; you don't plan for adulation, there's no decision. My work is also a message of freedom, because I could never understand why women were criticized so much over the height of their heels. I freed up the concept of the very high heel, and today women dare to wear them.

When I was little, I wanted to work for cabaret dancers. My fantasies all centered on them, and I always managed to slip into the Folies Bergère for free, or some of the other places. I would watch the same show day after day, and seeing it again always made it appear different. Each time I would discover new details that had escaped me before.

I like cabaret dancers because they are birds of paradise, with all those feathers, all those costume jewels… But I also like a Brigitte Bardot or an Audrey Hepburn, who both had extraordinary grace and modernity in ballerina flats (another dancer's shoe!).

I love the world of the "little ladies of Paris" and of exotic Parisiennes like Norma Duval and Farida. To be a Parisian woman is a matter of soul, whatever your birthplace.

Arletty is completely a woman of Paris, whereas Catherine Deneuve strikes me more as a French woman.

In the collective unconscious, Louboutin is synonymous with high heels. But you have designed many other types of shoes.

It's better to be envied than to be pitied! Heels symbolize shoes at a very high level; when you think of women's shoes, you think of heels. But I also adore flats.

I defend high heels and the femininity that they allow. Women who like high heels are neither bimbos nor sluts—anyway, I've never understood this discourse inherited from the 1970s according to which a woman who is pretty, feminine, and who wears makeup is necessarily a superficial woman.

It's a prerogative of women, which I uphold and which many men certainly envy them for. The image of the "lovely airhead" which gained currency in the 1950s and 1960s—in part from the movies—is completely obsolete, and, besides, no one has ever convinced me that an excess of femininity and beauty ever hurt someone's intelligence! I find it a very reductive and old-fashioned way of thinking. Femininity is interesting; women are right to make use of it.

Look at Tina Turner: independent, divorced, picking up her career again, not needing anyone. Remember how sexy she was in a form-fitting dress and super-high heels! And Blondie? She arrived as a bleached blonde, wearing red lipstick and mules, taking ownership of her femininity in a predominantly male rock-and-roll world. She became an icon. Who today would question her talent or her artistic commitment?

Does a French woman wear heels in a particular way?

Yes, but it's because she has more choices. Parisian women belong to the city. They are unfaithful to their suppliers, because they face multiple temptations; they wear no uniform, as in certain countries. Parisian women mix and combine jackets, shoes, perfumes, handbags…

Do you favor Marlene Dietrich over Marilyn?

I like Marilyn as much as Marlene. A perfect shoe would be two-headed: Marlene from in front for the elegance of her crossed legs, and Marilyn from behind for her walk.

Your favorite film: *The Barefoot Contessa*, by Mankiewicz, or *High Heels*, by Almodóvar?

I prefer *Pandora* [and the *Flying Dutchman*], with Ava Gardner, and especially *Cat People*, by Jacques Tourneur. And *Mademoiselle*, with Jeanne Moreau.

The first pair of Louboutins a woman should buy for herself?

A pump, the four-and-a-half-inch Showcase to start with.

. . . .

"Femininity is interesting; women are right to make use of it."

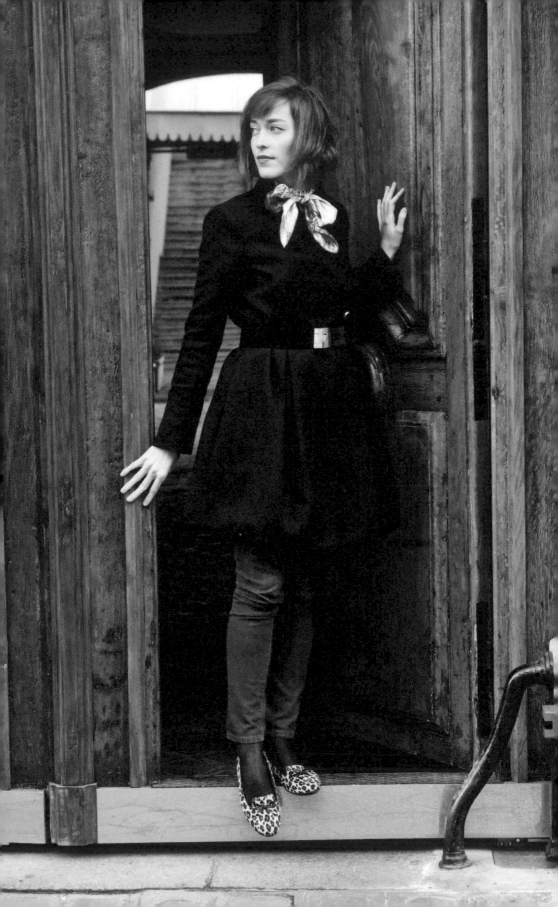

BALLET FLATS,
THE LBD OF FOOTWEAR

They are the little black dress of footwear—the shoe that every woman should own because it adapts to every item in her wardrobe. The truth is that high heels don't always define sex appeal.

Ballet flats, which are now everywhere, were once worn only by dancers. They came into their own thanks to two actresses who abandoned the popular style embodied by the other Hollywood stars of the 1950s.

In 1953, Audrey Hepburn was shooting *Roman Holiday*. She asked Ferragamo, shoemaker to the stars, to make her a pair of light ballerinas, mounted on low heels, so as to highlight her dancer's silhouette. This William Wyler film was a success, Hepburn won an Oscar, and ballet flats were on their way to glory.

· ·

"I bought these ballet flats on an impulse while wandering around Paris in late September. It was mild, sunny weather, and I was wearing shoes that made my feet hot."

Esther Bonté, scarf designer, in Geox ballet flats

In 1956, Roger Vadim made ... *and God Created Woman*, and the same year Brigitte Bardot spurred on the popularity of ballet flats by asking Repetto to make her a light and elegant style. And so the Cinderella was born, deeply scooped, making the foot highly sensual. It has never since lost its popularity and is still manufactured today, largely in Repetto's workshops in the Périgord region, to the tune of six thousand pairs a day!

With these two pairs of flat, girlish shoes, a new way of being sexy came into being!

All the designers were soon offering their version of this shoe: In 1962, Roger Vivier designed a ballerina flat with a square buckle for Yves Saint Laurent, which Catherine Deneuve made famous in *Belle de Jour*, directed by Luis Buñuel.

Another famous ballet flat, launched by Chanel in 1957 as a two-toned shoe (because beige lengthens the leg and a black tip shortens the foot), still appears in Chanel's collections.

WHO PUT THE BALLET IN THE FLAT?

The ballet flat as we know it today made its first appearance in London in 1932, when Jacob Bloch, a ballet aficionado, developed a comfortable slipper for ballerinas. His shoe, inspired by the flat-heeled pumps of the day, quickly caught the fancy of all the best dancers. This type of flat, open-topped pump had existed for several centuries and was worn by both men and women of high society.

In the beginning of the nineteenth century, women often wore them laced with ribbons around their ankles. They were made of silk so fine that they wore out after a single ball. European women wore them throughout the nineteenth century—sometimes embroidered, swathed in ribbons, or decorated with lace and precious stones—when proper women did not yet wear heels, which were considered too vulgar.

HOW DO YOU CHOOSE A PAIR OF BALLET FLATS?

Be careful, because not all ballerinas are the real thing. True ballerinas, entirely chic and so *French*, are the ones modeled on dance slippers, with a little bow in front for tightening the lace around the whole shoe. The ones with reinforced rubber edges, decorative stitching, and straps on top are not!

We like them made of fabric, leather, patent leather, or kidskin. Forget the ones that are shoddily manufactured or made of cheap materials, because they will look ratty in no time. Go for colors and animal prints; a leopard ballerina can revamp even the most classic look.

While fashionistas may not be promoting them right now, ballerinas continue to make their way out the door of the Repetto boutique on the rue Royale, next to the Paris Opera. You see them in all brands at the gates to high schools and the entrances to office buildings. The ballet flat has become a timeless staple; it's practical, and it goes with everything.

SOMETIMES IT CAN GO TOO FAR… BE CAREFUL!

In the eyes of Fred Marzo, the shoe designer, ballerinas are shoes. Which is to say that they're not slippers. "They must have a minimum amount of structure to be chic. If they lose their shape too quickly, the foot takes over, and it's rarely pretty."

Opposite:
Hot pink Repetto
ballet flats

Proof that ballet flats still have mystique?

Hedi Slimane, artistic director of Yves Saint Laurent since March 2012, is offering a new ballerina named Dance, which is an adaptation of ballet slippers for civilian use, following in the tradition of one of the great couturier's classics.

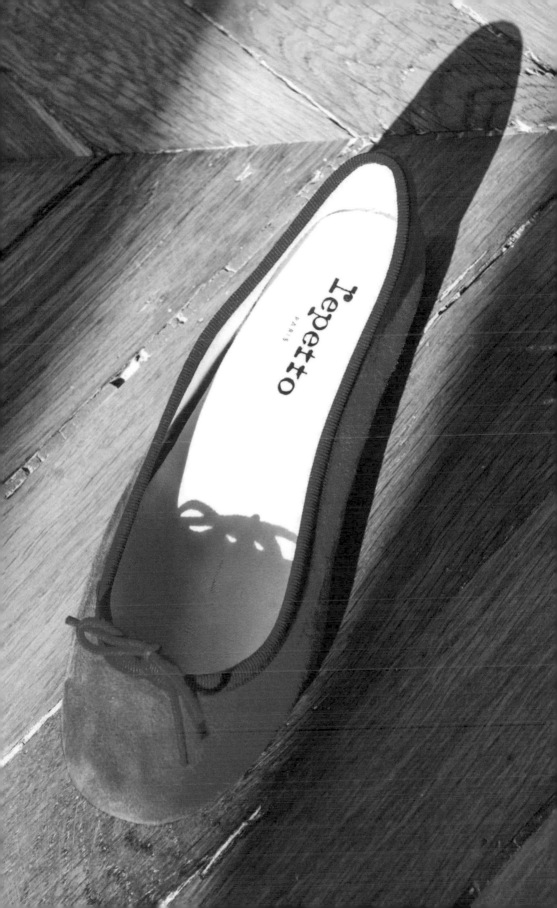

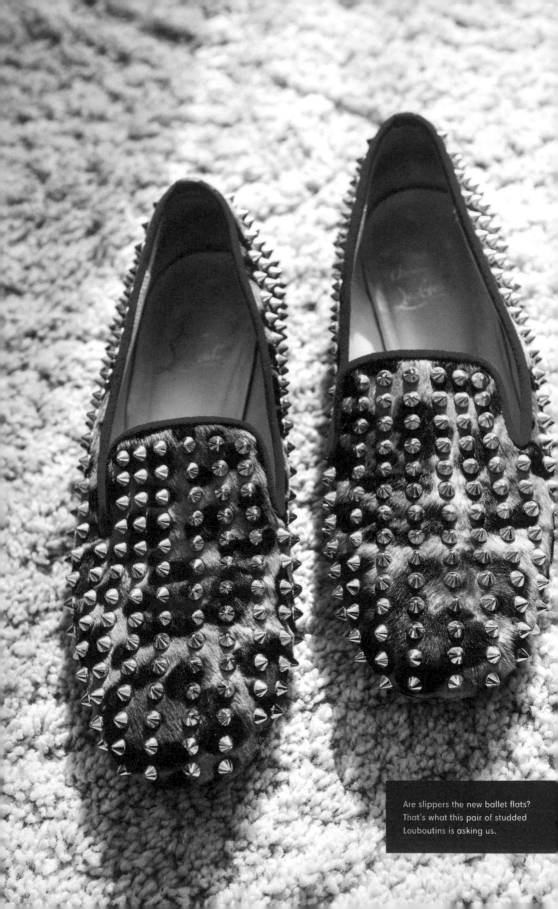

Are slippers the new ballet flats? That's what this pair of studded Louboutins is asking us.

They can be worn with practically everything, from denim shorts to chinos to a flared skirt. Unless you have long legs, avoid wearing them with a wide or straight trouser, and always show some ankle to lengthen your legs.

Needless to say, the ballerina's thin, flat sole makes it a shoe for dressing up, not for wearing on a forced march!

HOW LOW-CUT SHOULD A BALLERINA BE?

Whether it's flat as a pancake or incorporates a low heel, we like it very low-cut, to the point where it shows the base of the toes, which lengthens your foot. "But you have to make sure that they stay on your feet well," says Marzo.

Even though the low cut is one of the obvious features of a ballet flat, it isn't to everyone's taste. Some women hate to show toe cleavage: "It's indecent." "I have a prominent bone there, and it looks ugly." If that's true, you need to know your little anatomical flaws and work with them.

In any case, be sure that the sole is extremely thin, "with a tiny little heel for comfort!" says Marzo. And avoid rubber soles that extend beyond the upper (the part of the shoe that covers the toes, the top of the foot, the sides of the foot, and the back of the heel).

As very flat shoes have a tendency to flatten the foot, stay away from crossed elastic straps that make you look as if you're wearing little girl's shoes in a size eleven and a half.

CAN THEY BE UNFLATTERING?

Yes, if you wear them with a wide trouser or a long skirt. Less so if they are low-cut and worn with skinny jeans or cropped pants that show your ankle.

Ballerinas also work well with a knee-length dress, a miniskirt, or shorts.

If you're in any doubt, think of Brigitte Bardot in ... and God Created Woman, think of Audrey Hepburn, think of Jean Seberg. Their way of wearing ballerinas will never go out of fashion.

A FEW NUMBERS

It's claimed that Queen Marie Antoinette had more than five hundred pairs of these slippers, which a servant was responsible for maintaining and arranging by color and style. A pair of these delicate silk shoes once belonging to Marie Antoinette was sold at auction in October 2012 at the Hôtel Drouot in Paris for €62,460, or $84,567.

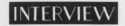

Olivier Jault

SHOE DESIGNER FOR REPETTO

· · · · · · · · · · · · · · · · · · ·

1947: *At the urging of her son, the dancer Roland Petit, Rose Repetto designed her first pair of dance slippers.*

1956: *At the request of Brigitte Bardot, Repetto created the Cinderella ballerina flat. And in the most scandalous scene in Roger Vadim's …and God Created Woman, Bardot wore an unforgettable pair of crimson patent leather Cinderellas.*

1970: *By chance, in a bargain bin, Jane Birkin found a pair of shoes that, as she thought, would be kind to the very delicate feet of Serge Gainsbourg. It was a pair of the famous Zizis, which Rose Repetto designed for her daughter-in-law Zizi Jeanmaire. Gainsbourg tried them on and never took them off. He became an ambassador for the brand.*

2000s: *Repetto entered into partnerships with some of the great designers—Issey Miyake, Yohji Yamamoto, Karl Lagerfeld, and Comme des Garçons, which has designed a ballerina with studs.*

2012: *Repetto opened its trade school in leatherworking. Its goal is to teach its students to turn out a ballerina in the "stitch-and-return" technique in six months.*

Today: *Repetto makes five hundred thousand pairs of ballet flats each year in its factory in the Dordogne. There's no stopping a symbol!*

How do you explain the perennial popularity of the ballet flat?

It is a "transgenerational" shoe. Invisible and at the same time a presence. Comfortable, with an easy elegance: You can wear it with a pair of narrow jeans as well as with a frilly skirt. When you're fifteen and when you're seventy-five. More than anything, it's a shoe that contributes actively to the youthfulness of a woman's appearance. It gives you a "young look." What woman doesn't want that? And of the twenty-five shades of color that we offer, pink systematically outperforms the others.

What makes a ballet flat distinctive?

The definition boils down to a single word: lightness. A ballerina should be an extension of the foot. A glove for the foot. And this is true for all

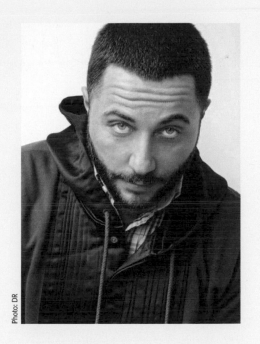

Photo: DR

· ·

Hurray for the custom shoe trend!

With 252 different gradations of lambskin, different colors for the trim, upper, and laces, each woman can dream up her very own pair of Cinderella flats. Oops! Personalization comes at a price: €320 ($435)…

· ·

three heights of uppers that we offer. Ballerinas are not sexual, but they are sexy. Lightness is a more interesting way to embody sexiness, no? And just like the little black dress, what's hard to achieve is this simplicity. The quality of the leather, made in France for Repetto, along with our famous "stitch-and-return" technique, count for a lot.

Where do you draw fresh inspiration?

Repetto isn't a "fashionable" shoemaker. You're never going to find us selling moon boots! We offer timeless styles, staying faithful to our DNA: dance. From classical, to tango, to salsa, to waltz, to hip-hop… the range of possibilities is enormous. From ballet flats to ballroom sandals, and not forgetting sneakers. A few years ago, I thought we needed a moccasin and designed the famous Michael. By chance, Kate Moss bought a pair in black patent leather, had herself photographed in them, and suddenly all the girls wanted them. Don't worry, I have other ideas in reserve!

LET IT SPARKLE!

Sometimes a woman feels like sprinkling her shoes with pixie dust. Not so she can run faster, and not to find Prince Charming (although…), but just to give her feet a more festive look—to make the pavement less gray.

On the catwalks for Fall/Winter 2011–2012, a number of designers—Miu Miu, Versace, Marc Jacobs—made women's eyes shine by showing big heels sheathed in multicolored spangles. Whether an homage to the red shoes Dorothy wore in *The Wizard of Oz* or to the shimmering disco years, it brought glitter back into the frame. But this time, it's not just for the dance floor, a jazz dance class, or on party nights—now sparkly shoes can be worn during the day, to a business lunch or on the bus. Every brand has since followed suit, from the great names in fashion to the discount retailers. And no one bats an eye if a businesswoman's pumps or a prim pair of Mary Janes sparkle like a thousand suns.

All over the Web you can find instructions for how to brighten an ordinary pair of boots by adding beading to the heels, or giving new life to a pair of worn sneakers with a shower of glitter. It's probably no coincidence that metallic gold and silver shoes have started taking over our shoe closets. Although they were once limited to the shelves for evening sandals and chic gladiators, they have now inserted themselves even among the most staid and fantasy-resistant shoes. You now see even brogues—those austere male shoes so perfect for the preppy look—in shiny gold.

Whether golden or glittering, the intent is the same: to tweak the classics and give some lilt to an outfit that would otherwise be dull. It's the perfect response to a day when you are feeling low or lacking in sartorial ambition.

The equation that takes a classic style and adds a dash of humor has every chance of surviving beyond many seasonal fads. But you have to want the adventure that sparkle suggests.

- - - - - - - - - - - - - - - -

"I wear size eleven-and-a-half, and I've actually bought shoes that were too small for me—and therefore unwearable—just because I wanted to own them."

Madjissem Beringaye, producer, in an Acne dress, trench coat by & Other Stories, Céline bag, gold metallic boots by George Esquivel

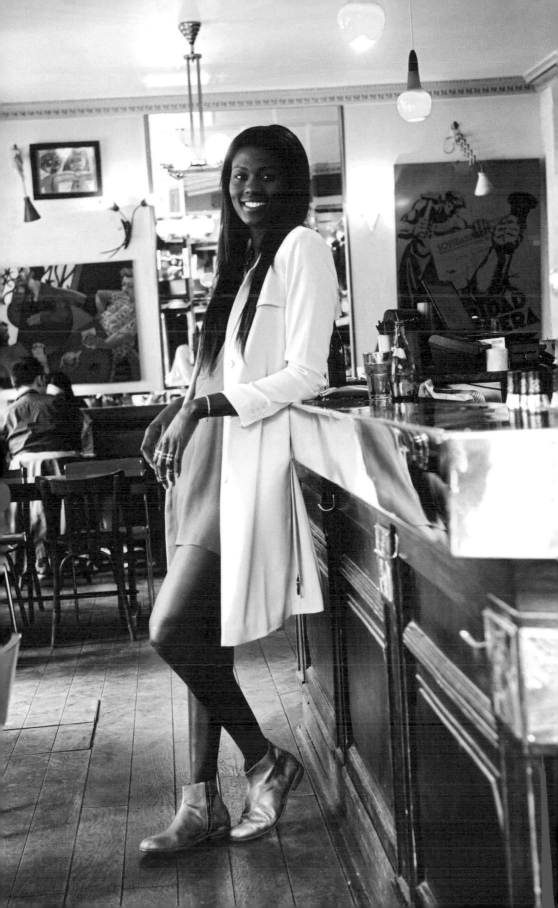

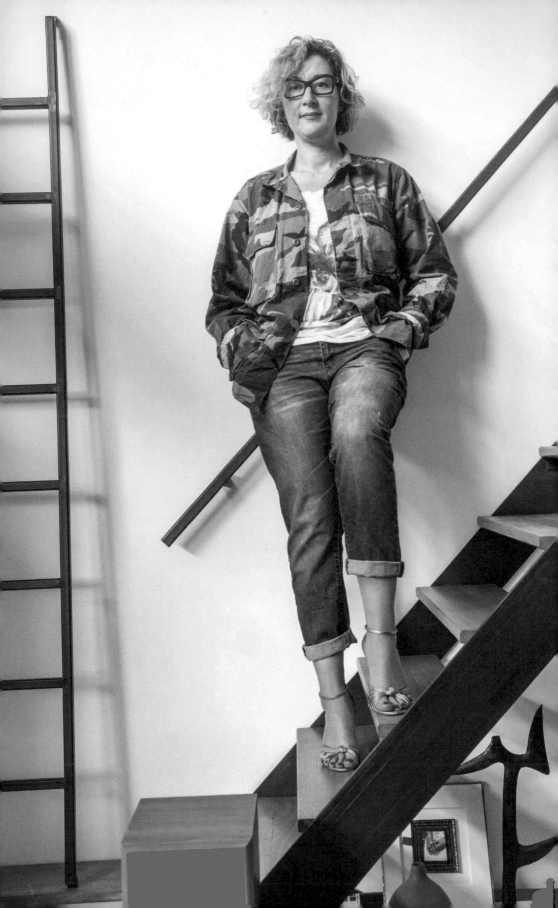

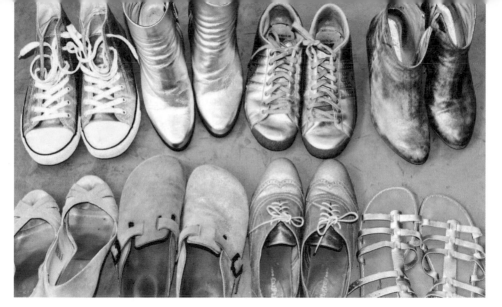

"It's a weekend outfit but made dressier by the sandals; if I change the military jacket for a white tuxedo jacket, I can go to the office—maybe not to see just any clients, but the ones that are sensitive to fashion."

Emmanuelle Messéan de Sélorges, communications consultant, in a surplus military jacket by Doursoux, t-shirt by The Kooples, boyfriend jeans by Gap, Pura Lopez sandals

HOW SHOULD YOU CHOOSE YOUR GOLD OR SPARKLY SHOES?

➡ If you're afraid that people will look only at your feet (it feels strange at first, but you get used to it!), then lower the risk with a two-stage shoe. For instance, one with suede on the front and discreet beading on the back, or a shoe with only one bold element such as on the heel of a pump, the ankle strap of a sandal, or the toe of a ballerina.

➡ No need to muddy the waters; choose styles that are plain and straightforward. Select an oxford, a sandal, or a pair of classic pumps over fancier shoes or high-heeled boots.

➡ Avoid extra flourishes—spikes, multiple straps, two-inch platforms—that might obscure the otherwise elegant bling of your pretty shoes. Again, the basic form should be simple.

➡ Make the distinction between a thin coat of sparkly paint and a layer of sequins: The first, of course, is more discreet and can be worn almost anywhere. It can even go nearly unnoticed if it matches the shoe's suede or leather.

➡ When it comes to metallic finishes, pay attention to the fine gradations. As with jewelry, it's best not to choose gold in Bollywood yellow or 24-carat, oriental-palace range. Opt instead for something at the coppery or bronze end of the spectrum, or an older gold with patina. It's less flashy and therefore more chic.

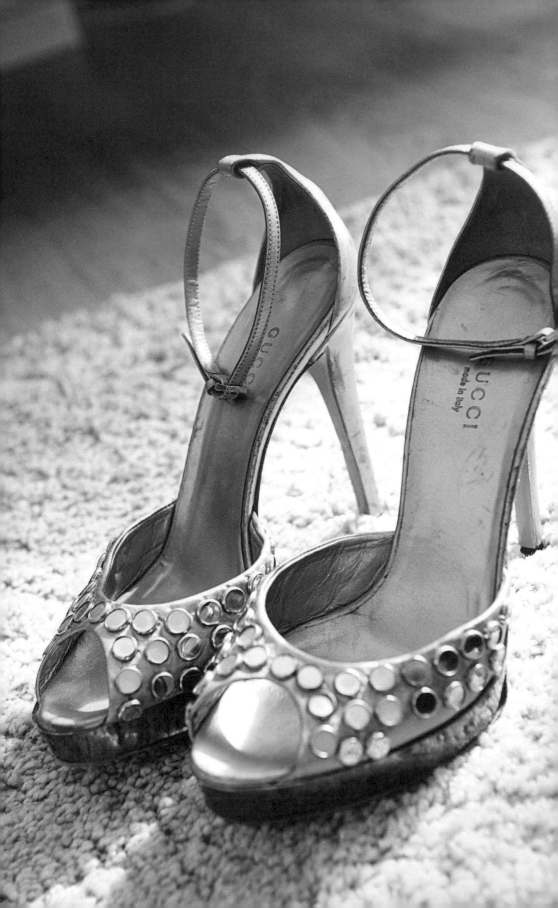

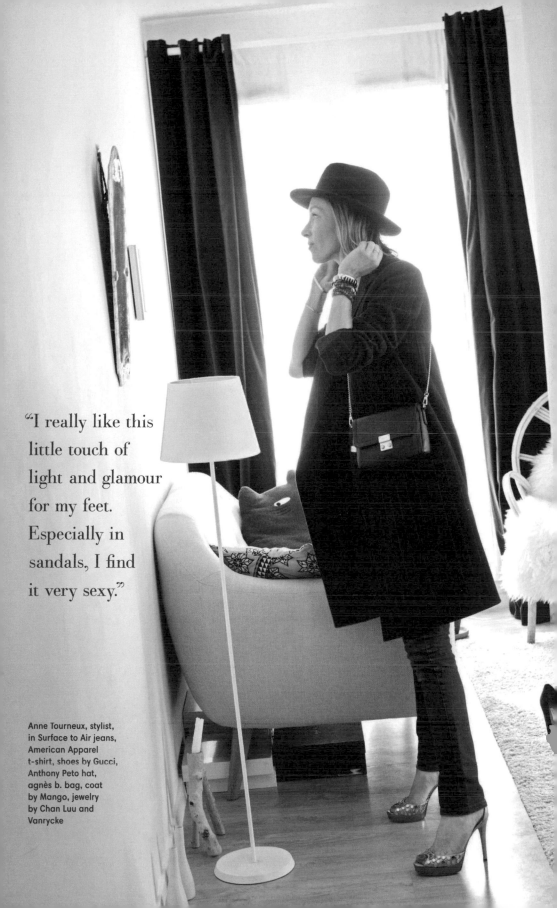

"I really like this little touch of light and glamour for my feet. Especially in sandals, I find it very sexy."

Anne Tourneux, stylist, in Surface to Air jeans, American Apparel t-shirt, shoes by Gucci, Anthony Peto hat, agnès b. bag, coat by Mango, jewelry by Chan Luu and Vanrycke

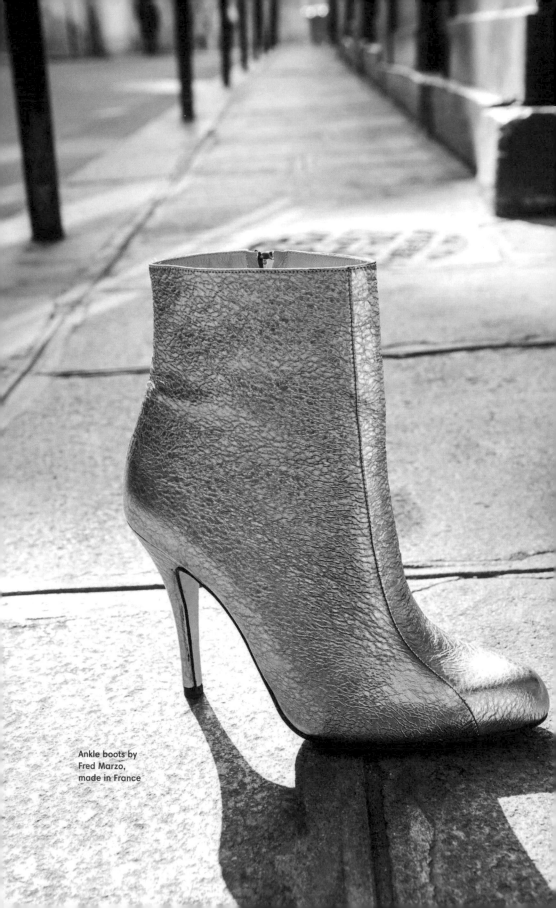

Ankle boots by
Fred Marzo,
made in France

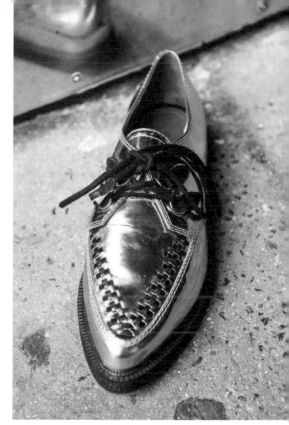

Creepers by Underground

WHAT TO WEAR THEM WITH?

Whether you choose gold or sparkles, you are never too old to shine. In contrast to what you might think, mastering these "jewel shoes" is extremely easy. We aren't afraid to say that "they go with everything"! Worn on tanned feet in summertime, over wool socks in winter, or with semi-opaque tights (charcoal, navy, gray, or ecru), they transcend any particular look.

Even if the shoes in your closet are extreme and futuristic, don't be afraid! You'll find that they go with any number of outfits for day or night. Instead of leaving them on the shelf, wear them as if it were no big deal. To start off, we recommend pairing them with jeans and a t-shirt. Simplicity is the best gambit. Oh really, there are sequins on my running shoes? Little by little, you'll find that you can wear them with other items in your wardrobe without any fear of striking a wrong note.

➡ **If you are shy, pair them with a basic outfit:**
- Jeans + heather gray t-shirt + metallic gold oxfords
- Off-white chinos + navy pea jacket + boots with sparkly heels
- Cropped pants + tunic + metallic gold ballet flats
- A little summer dress in ecru cotton voile + glittery sandals

➡ **Try matching them with prints or more sophisticated clothes:**
- A flowered print dress + gold Mary Janes
- A checkered trouser + blue-jean shirt + glittery oxfords

- Deep green leather shorts + tank top + gold sandals
- A beige pencil dress + gold pumps

➡ **Subtler than when paired with black,** gold picks up all the tints of pinkish beige, camel, chestnut, gray, khaki, navy, and burgundy.

➡ **It goes without saying that you shouldn't wear your shimmering shoes with another flashy item** (rhinestone-studded sweater, sequined skirt) or you'll get that carnival look—step right up, ladies and gentlemen, every player is a winner! Too much flash kills the sparkle.

You can also try metallic silver. The instruction booklet is the same; it's just a matter of taste.

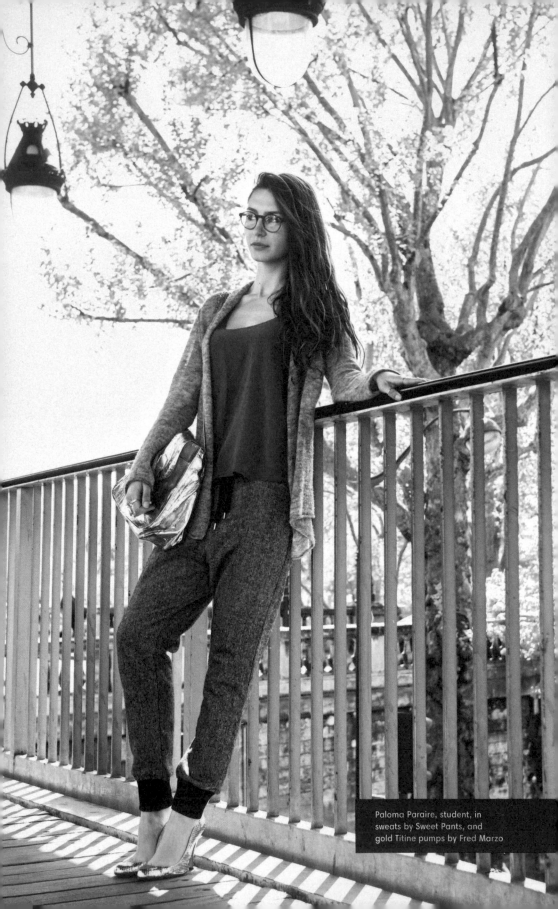

Paloma Paraire, student, in sweats by Sweet Pants, and gold Titine pumps by Fred Marzo

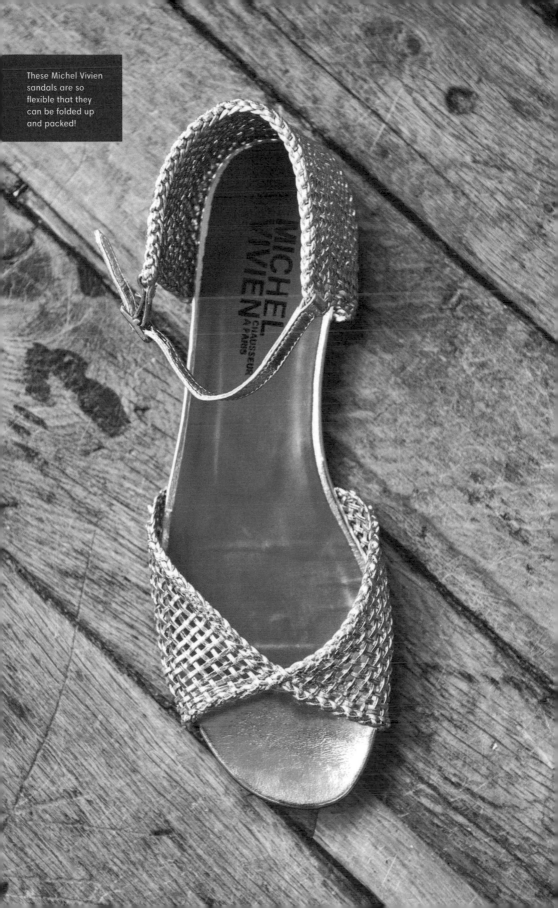

These Michel Vivien sandals are so flexible that they can be folded up and packed!

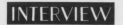

Mathilde Toulot

JOURNALIST AND FOUNDER OF THE BLOG *SHOOOOES*

In the US, people covet the dream shoes that fill the astonishing shoe closet of fiery redhead Jane Aldridge, author of the blog Sea of Shoes. In France, we love the sprightly prose and exemplary shoe shelves of Mathilde Toulot.

· · · · · · · · · · · · · · · · · ·

When did you fall in love with shoes?

As far back as I can remember, I've always had a heart flutter for shoes. But it's impossible to say what I'm projecting onto them that I should love them as much as I do. My favorite activity as a little girl? Asking my grandmother (whose best friend was head seamstress at Dior and made her haute couture dresses in her spare time!) to lend me shoes from her very special collection of Charles Jourdans, so that I could go on "walks" down the garden paths wearing these astonishing high heels. I wasn't simply admiring their shapes or practicing to walk. What I liked best was telling myself the stories that went along with them: How each shoe was an attribute of a strong and powerful woman. A woman who was active, dominant, with a place in the world. Have I always associated shoes with power? Hello, is this my shrink?

How do you explain the addiction that women feel toward shoes?

It's completely psychoanalytic, not to say fetishistic. Shoes are rich in symbols and carry our relation to seduction, self-affirmation, femininity (is wearing heels about being a strong woman or a fragile one?). This heel, which is long and pointed like a phallus… I hate clichés, but all the same it's interesting to look at. And then, they're easy to buy, they're cute, they're an accessory so there's less anxiety than about a dress. No matter what your shoe size, you have lots of options. It's playful; it changes your whole outfit in the blink of an eye.

Are you typically in flats or up on stilts?

I adore high heels, but I *adore* my freedom even more. I hate being constrained. I recently found myself thinking something that consoled me for not wearing heels every day: When I wear skyscraper heels, my body is unstable and has to work to keep its balance. My brain is forced to concentrate nonstop on this useless task. And when you add the pain in my feet, I have no room to think of anything else. Aren't there better uses for my time and my little gray cells? Yes!

When you fall in love with a shoe, how do you justify it?

There are very few that I'm going to do the deed with. I'm not a compulsive buyer at all (sometimes I'd like to be a little crazier!). My purchases are carefully considered and narrowly

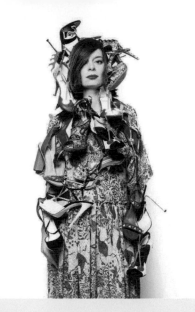

"How can you tell a good shoe? By the sequins! No, I'm joking."

· · · · · · · · · · · · · · · · · · · ·

targeted. But I also know that when I'm under-going a period of anxiety, I'm more prone to making impulse buys. My Church['s] oxfords are an example. Luckily, even at those times, I seem to make useful purchases...

Do you know what is going to make you fall in love with a shoe?

The combination of practicality and cuteness! My low-heeled Yves Saint Laurent pumps with a beaded red bow from the Summer/Spring 2014 collection are a good example.

What's the style that is most often duplicated on your shoe shelf?

Black ankle boots. I'm like Madame Bovary when it comes to shoes: never satisfied. I'm always looking for the ideal pair of black ankle boots.

Are there shoes that you never wear?

To my great regret, the forty pairs of evening shoes that sit in my shoe closet. Not enough occasions for them, and also what I said earlier about liking to feel free.

What makes a beautiful shoe?

It has to do more than anything with craftmen-ship. A sharp line made actual in the hands of an excellent designer, a selection of top-of-the-line materials... Ugly plastic and bits of glue bulging out—even if the shoe is nice, I'll find it unacceptable because I'm such a maniac!

High heels that don't hurt your feet—do they exist?

There are no comfortable high heels; it's all a lie. Or mind over matter.

The contemporary shoe designers that we should keep an eye on...

The French are doing well. There's Amélie Pichard, Fred Marzo, Olivia Cognet at Apologie, Thomas Lieuvin (the kid in the bunch). And I'm very taken with Flamingos, a company started by Anne Blum, who's worked as an agent for the great shoemakers for the past twenty years.

On the international scene, there are three in the lead pack: Charlotte Olympia, Nicholas Kirkwood, and Tabitha Simmons. In the too-too-British style, there's Sophia Webster. And on the opposite end, the king is Francesco Russo.

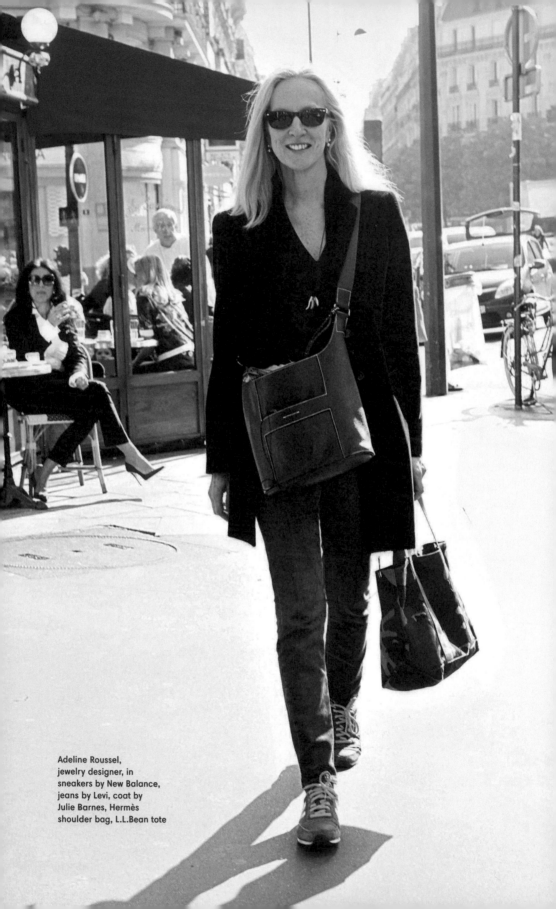

Adeline Roussel,
jewelry designer, in
sneakers by New Balance,
jeans by Levi, coat by
Julie Barnes, Hermès
shoulder bag, L.L.Bean tote

BEING CHIC IN SNEAKS

It took forty years for sneakers to make their way from the streets of Harlem to the Chanel Haute Couture Spring/Summer 2014 show. It was the hip-hop movement that first brought them off the sports field, and soon they were being worn by break-dancers. No shoe is better for dancing on pavement or rapping on stage, or for giving yourself style with (almost) no effort!

As the official shoe of the rappers of the 1980s, athletic shoes were worn with customized laces and a Kangol hat. No self-respecting rapper ventured out without a toothbrush to wipe away scuff marks and keep the shoes immaculate and gleaming. When Run DMC's hit single, "My Adidas," was met with worldwide success in 1986, the band signed the first non-sport sponsoring contract with the company for $1 million. Sales exploded. After that, every maker of athletic shoes wanted its piece of the pie. Nike paired with Heavy D, Converse with Busy Bee, and Fila with Fresh Gordon, because each wanted its own rap group to promote sales. But it was Nike that won really big when it bet on a young basketball player, Michael Jordan, who would propel the Air Jordan to the top of the hype heap. The shoe's astonishing success gave Nike the idea of issuing limited editions. Sneakers became an obsession for some collectors. You can get a sense of the inflated prices of some of these shoes by taking a brief tour of eBay, where a pair of twentieth-anniversary Reebok Pumps, for instance, was recently being offered for $3,999.99.

Nowadays, sneakers have only a marginal association with sports, so widely have they been accepted into urban fashion.

While working girls of the 1990s in New York were still wearing them as back-up shoes for

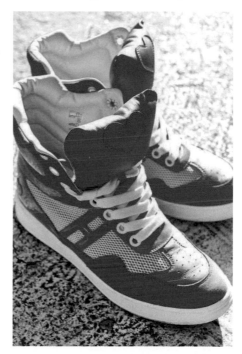

Hogan by Katie Grand

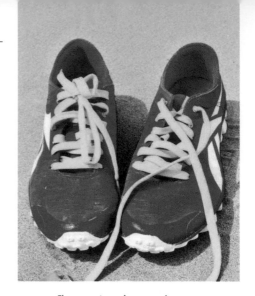

Fluorescent sneakers can give some
pop to a low-key outfit

use on Manhattan's sidewalks, French women were already sensing the fashion potential of this accessory. They didn't just wear New Balance shoes à la Bill Clinton for comfort and convenience, they carefully picked their style: the Gazelle or Stan Smith by Adidas, the Nike Waffle, the Converse All Star, Vans' Era.... Each woman could pick a team. And it didn't matter if you changed playing fields often. Fashion is a place where being unfaithful is OK.

More than anything, French women have a different way of wearing sneakers. It's not about hip-hop or saying "my feet are tired of heels." It's an alternate approach that incorporates a pinch of dissonance, a touch of chic, and a hint of bourgeois affluence. The incursion of athletic gear into a sophisticated outfit allows French women to pull off that effortless look at which they are unparalleled. Yes, they work at their effect. But they still manage to be cool. In a man's coat and carrying a Carven clutch, they can stay—thanks to their running shoes—just this side of a too-calculated elegance.

Are French women sophisticated or are they casual? Neither. They know just how to blend these two extremes: fishnet tights + Reeboks, Prince of Wales plaid + Stan Smiths, chiffon + Converse All Stars...

SHOULD YOU WEAR DESIGNER SNEAKERS?

Chanel, Martin Margiela, Dior, Isabel Marant, Louis Vuitton, Kanye West—it's easy to find sneakers carrying the stamp of a big fashion name such as the famous limited-edition Colorama issued by Pierre Hardy in 2008. The shoe sold out immediately and became a cult item on everyone's list. The designer has obliged the public ever since by producing a new version each season.

Sophisticated details (wedge heels, embroidery, beading) reassuringly mark sneakers as high fashion to the regular consumer. But bolder fashionistas like to shop for sneakers in sporting goods stores. No need to search designer collections for them and pay designer prices; plus, you get the benefit of all the high-performance technology that's been packed into these little marvels: flexible sole, good cushioning, maximum air flow, optimal weight... You just have to remember them on the days when you're not jogging!

"I don't often wear heels, I travel around Paris on a bike. Wearing heels on a bike, you really feel like a grasshopper!"

Adeline Roussel

. . . .

WORKING SNEAKERS INTO YOUR WARDROBE

Sure, they're not the most elegant shoes. Who cares? Being chic doesn't always call for serious glamour. You have the right to have fun, too.

➡ Wearing a tracksuit or jeans is cheating. Take advantage of your sneakers' fashion aura to refresh your wardrobe or give a note of fantasy to a classic look.

Example: navy wool trousers + blouse + colored Nikes.

➡ To look chic, pair your running shoes with well-tailored and good-quality clothes. Forget about the grunge sweater and faded jeans if you're over twenty-five.

Example: sober blazer + gray V-necked cashmere pullover + ankle-length pants + Stan Smiths.

➡ Don't be afraid to wear them on a night out. When meeting for drinks at a hip bar or joining friends for an informal dinner, sneakers can give an edge to a hyper-feminine outfit.

Example: t-shirt + leather pencil skirt + New Balances.

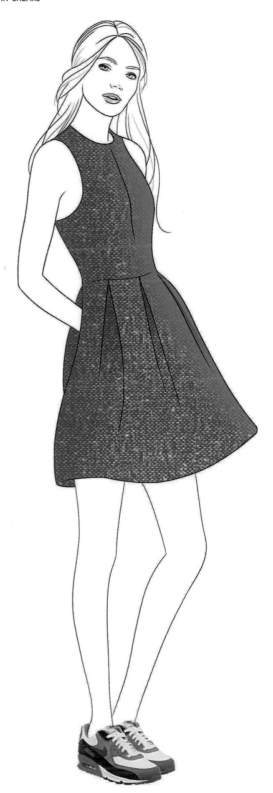

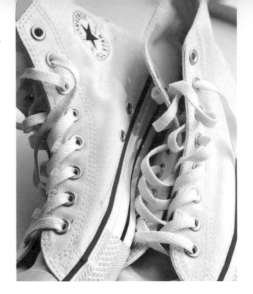

We all have (at least!) one pair of Converse
Chuck Taylor All Stars in our closet

DANGER!

➡ **White sneakers:** We don't know why, but
except for Stan Smiths and Chuck Taylors they
all remind us of what surgical interns wear.
Avoid a totally white-on-white shoe.

➡ **Metallic silver:** Avoid overdoing it unless you
want to field questions about alien sightings.
Pair them, for instance, with white chinos and
a pea jacket.

➡ **Beaded sneaks:** Yes, if you're wearing them
to give pep to an otherwise dull outfit, but don't
pair them with frayed mini-shorts and false
nails... unless you're trying out for a Missy Elliott
music video.

➡ **Animal motifs:** Leopard, tiger, snake... a
menagerie of animal motifs can be well suited
for nights out on the town. But keep it simple
and avoid wearing them with other vibrant
fabrics that might clash in combination. Less
is more.

Python slip-ons by Clarisse Virot

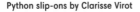

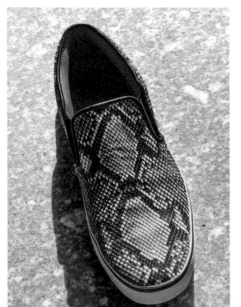

➡ **Black sneakers:** Oops, sorry, we just yawned!
Sneakers are meant to jazz up your appearance, not put it to sleep! Be bold, or revisit
sneakers later. Or not at all. No one says you
have to like them.

➡ **What about wedges?** There are two camps,
those violently for wedge sneakers and those
violently against them. Closer to an orthopedic shoe than to a ball slipper, the wedged
sneaker, popularized by Isabel Marant in 2008,
has been copied ad nauseam by a number of
lesser designers. Not easy to wear, it has a tendency to make the leg look stocky, as it hides
the ankle, its slenderest portion. Takeaway:
It's best used by slender, long-limbed women.
You've been warned!

· ·

*"Even though I love wearing
flats, sneakers especially, I
am comfortable with my
height. Sometimes, when I'm
wearing heels, I top out at
almost six-foot-seven."*

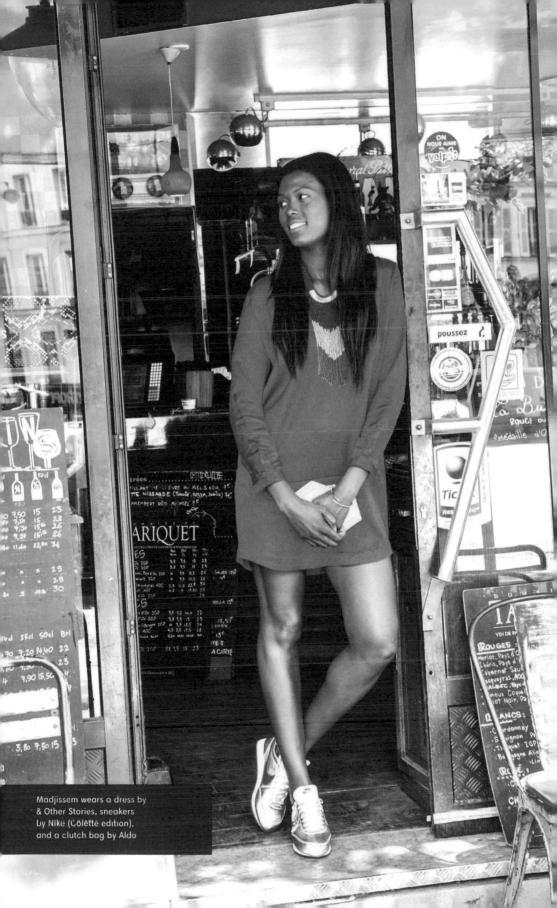

Madjissem wears a dress by
& Other Stories, sneakers
by Nike (Colette edition),
and a clutch bag by Aldo

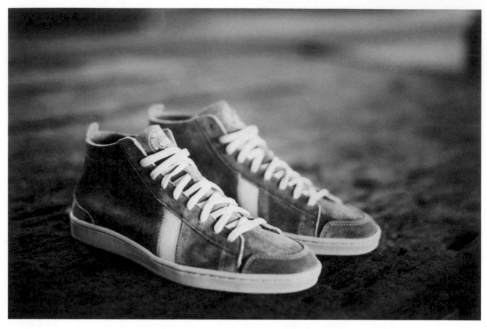

We are partial to Sawa Shoes, which are made in
Ethiopia from raw materials sourced entirely in Africa.

Caring for Your Sneakers

➡ To whiten the soles, consider using a toothbrush and toothpaste.

➡ To give luster to the leather, all you need is a little vegetable oil or a basic moisturizing cream.

➡ Don't hesitate to waterproof them before wearing. It will protect them from stains, and they'll be easier to clean.

➡ The white ones can be thrown into the washing machine.

A FEW DATES AND NUMBERS

1918: First appearance of the Converse All Star by Chuck Taylor.

1964: First appearance of Adidas's Stan Smith, reissued in 2013.

1973: First appearance of Puma's Clyde.

1984: First appearance of Nike's Air Jordan.

1989: First appearance of Reebok's Pump.

15 MILLION: The number of Nike Air Force Ones sold throughout the world in 2004.

2,000: The number of pairs owned by Damon Dash, sorted by brand and color—enough to wear a new pair every day for more than five years.

$30 BILLION: The annual revenue of the sneaker industry globally.

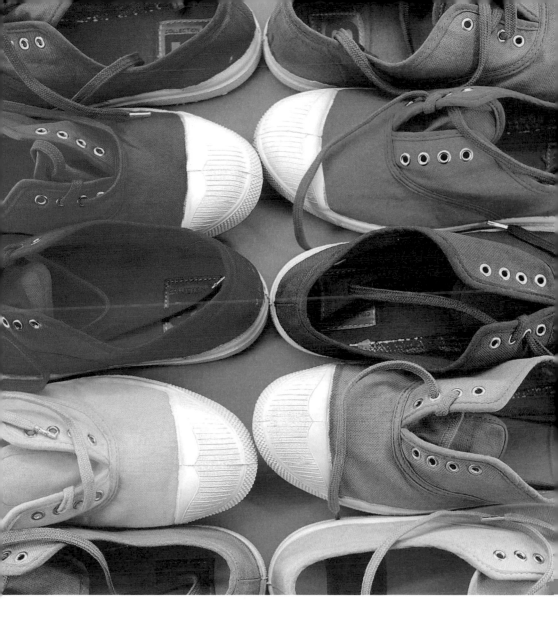

LA BENSIMON

These very French little sneakers first appeared in army gymnasiums but were appropriated in the 1980s by Serge Bensimon and soon started popping up in every Parisian woman's closet. The colored ones caught the fancy of the French editors of *Elle*, and the editors of women's fashion magazines all around the world soon followed suit. With its rubber sole and piece-dyed cotton uppers, it has undergone no alteration since its creation and is still manufactured in the same European factories. The Bensimon brand has more than six hundred thousand fans on Facebook. Its classic models come out in twenty colors every season, and there are limited editions, printed patterns, insulated models for winter wear, and co-editions with designers like Jean Paul Gaultier and Donna Karan. The Bensimon is quite simply for every generation, all seasons, and both sexes.

Pierre Hardy

SHOE DESIGNER

If a man looks at your legs insistently, it may be for a good reason.
After all, that's the charming tic of one of our favorite shoe designers.

. . . .

How did you become a shoe designer?
It happened by accident, because of drawing, which was my vocation. My Aunt Antoinette, a drawing teacher, discovered that I had talent and convinced my parents to let me explore this path. As a child, I would draw all summer. I imagined little figures, for whom I designed clothing, accessories, shoes. I drew them in India ink then painted them in watercolors.

When I started studying applied arts, I did a little of everything. From anatomy to architecture, I liked it all. When I finished studying, I decided to become a teacher so I wouldn't have to make a choice. It was the only profession I knew anyway, since both my parents were teachers.

Then, thanks to the people I met, I was commissioned to produce illustrations for *La Mode en peinture,* a superb magazine started by Prosper Assouline. And an agent friend got me work for different companies. One thing led to another, and I wound up at Dior.

It was the most famous fashion house in the world. But I was unaware of it... I oversaw licenses, shops, couture. I learned on the job about orchestrating themes, building a collection, doing research in the archives. Today, all of that seems obvious.

Your company is becoming more and more known; how do you see yourself developing?
I'd like to continue being a "fashion leader" and a commercial success—a hard thing to do! There are compromises I won't accept; that's how I live my life. I like the way Azzedine Alaïa manages his career, staying free. You know that the Pierre Hardy brand has to face off with companies with enormous means.

Shoes are an accessory that have to work on their own, that have to have their own fate.

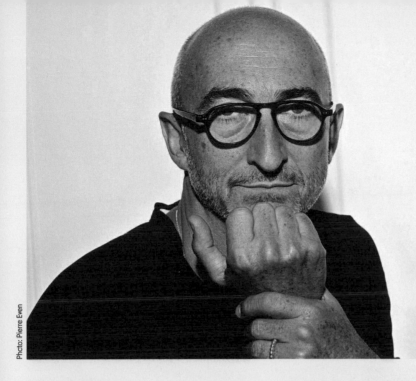

When you create a shoe, you are contributing to a small part of a person's figure.

Some shoes are made to disappear into a figure, others to make it stand out. I try to create a coherent object that isn't meant to be the simple extension of a clothing item. My shoes are designed for adventurous women, eccentric women—in the sense of "far from the center." The Pierre Hardy woman is sophisticated and wants something different. She knows how to set herself apart from uniformity. It's one of the reasons why I don't have a muse, because I am trying to describe a global aesthetic rather than bring it to life with a single woman.

Do you look at women's shoes in the street?
Yes, of course, their shoes and their legs. I look at women and the way they move.

I am sensitive to a lovely leg. A leg that is slightly thick doesn't offend me. Excessive slimness is not necessarily beautiful, but when the joints are slender, then I am moved.

As to heel height, I believe we've reached the limit! These extravagant heights make women walk in a disgraceful way.

How would you describe the French woman?
She is more fulfilled, more relaxed. She dresses for herself.

· · · · · · · · · · · · · · · · ·

"I didn't even know that it was a profession, creating shoes!"

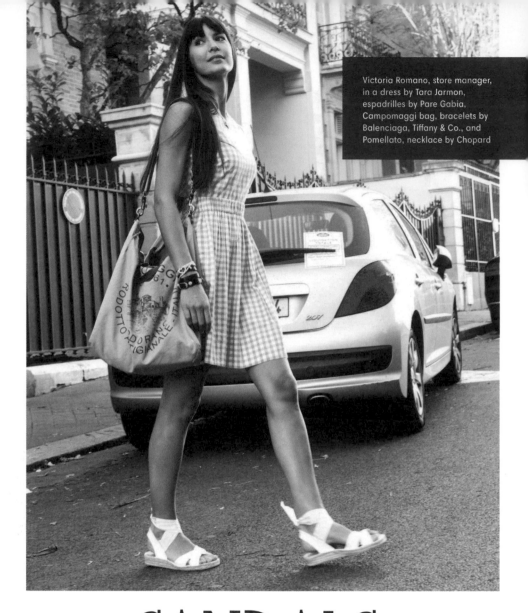

Victoria Romano, store manager, in a dress by Tara Jarmon, espadrilles by Pare Gabia, Campomaggi bag, bracelets by Balenciaga, Tiffany & Co., and Pomellato, necklace by Chopard

SANDALS,
FROM THE BEACH TO THE STREET

· · · · · · · · · · · · · · · · ·

A few straps, a leather sole… and there's all the promise of a summer night, tanned feet, a breath of freedom, and a reawakened sensuality. Ahh, if only life were always this simple!

"My sandals come from Rondini. I have them in several colors. I always wear them on vacation with every kind of outfit, and as soon as it gets nice and warm in Paris."

MARINA DE GAETANO, FINANCIAL COMPLIANCE OFFICER

Every civilization has made them after its own fashion and with its own materials: the Egyptians with papyrus, the Persians with wooden soles, the Spanish with rope. Roman matrons had them inset with precious stones or fine gold, and the Greek god Hermes traveled on winged sandals.

Long relegated to classical antiquity and the academic paintings of the nineteenth century—David's famous *Oath of the Horatii*, for instance—sandals reappeared at the beginning of the twentieth century and have had their place in wardrobes ever since. The flower-power generation made this open and previously immodest shoe, considered indecent until the 1940s, one of the emblems of the counterculture. Jackie Onassis entered legend wearing Canfora sandals, and even today this famous sandalmaker in Capri, Italy, honors her memory with its Like Jackie collection, which features the models most liked by the former first lady.

TIMELESS SANDALS

For their minimalism and superb elegance, we prefer finely crafted ones: The soles and straps made of leather, and the manufacturing done in France or Italy rather than India—more expensive, certainly, but also sturdier. The best known among them are Tropéziennes and Salomé, classic models by Rondini, sandalmakers in St. Tropez since 1927. Still produced in the atelier on the rue Georges-Clemenceau, a pair of genuine Tropéziennes is to French women

the ultimate sandal, often handed down from mother to daughter.

Sandals complement any and all summer outfits, even city wear, but the feet must be pumiced and the nails perfect. A pair of white jeans,

Sandal by Atelier Mercadal

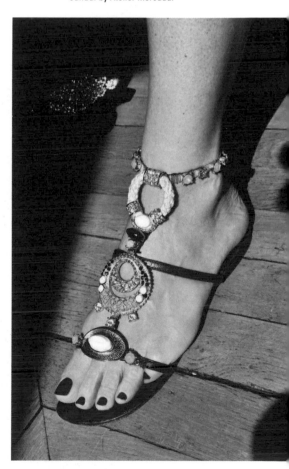

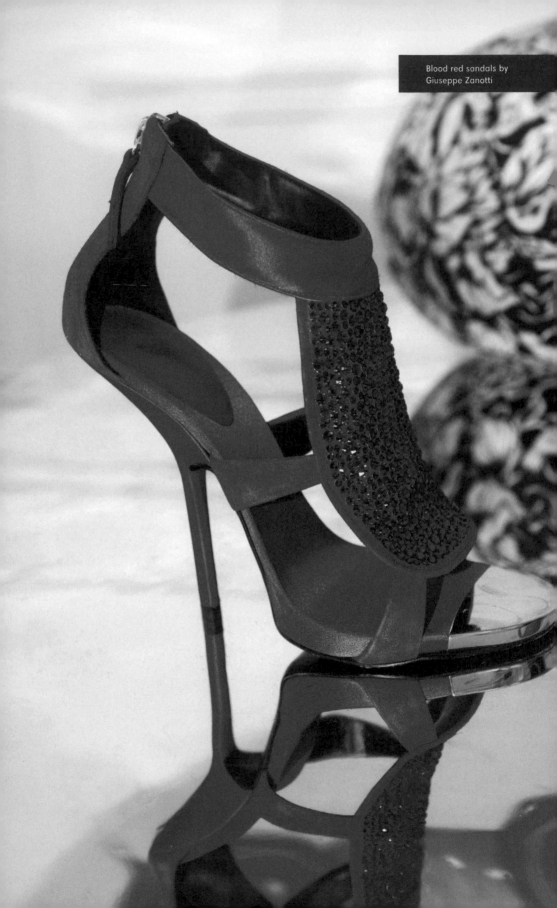

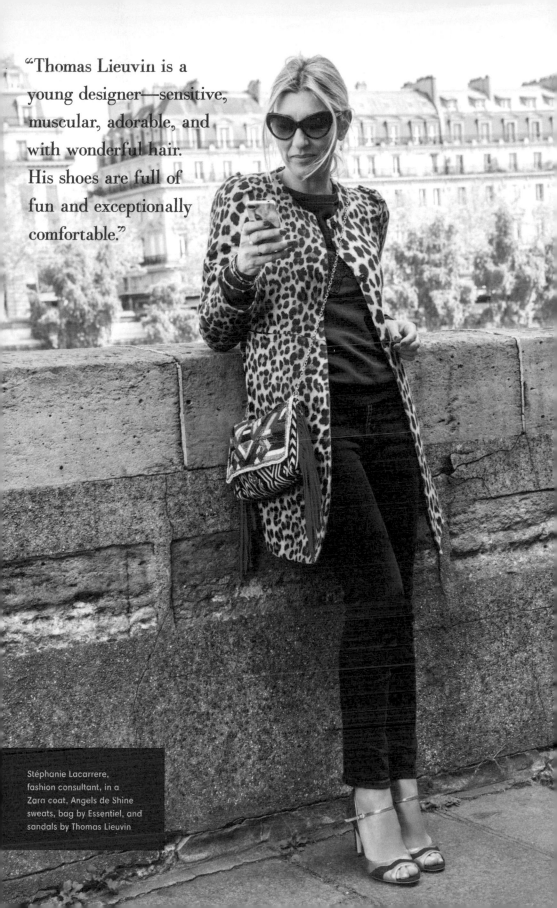

"Thomas Lieuvin is a young designer—sensitive, muscular, adorable, and with wonderful hair. His shoes are full of fun and exceptionally comfortable."

Stéphanie Lacarrere, fashion consultant, in a Zara coat, Angels de Shine sweats, bag by Essentiel, and sandals by Thomas Lieuvin

a swimsuit, an A-line dress, or denim shorts—nothing clashes with these icons of the summer wardrobe. Go for bright, bold colors, snakeskin patterns, a varnished finish: Your simple little dress or your worn jeans will only look smarter for it. You can also wear them with classic capris to give yourself a *Roman Holiday* allure. These cropped trousers from the 1960s were authoritatively rehabilitated by Christophe Decarnin, then head of Balmain, in 2009. You can probably guess that we favor gladiator sandals over pool slides, even in the upgraded 2014 versions!

THE ROAD TO COMPOSTELA

The abbey sandal has its aficionados—especially for those weary of showy designer logos. Directly inspired by the sandals crafted even today in certain convents and abbeys of France and Navarre, this style of sandal has inspired many designers, who have managed to infuse it with a measure of…spirituality? The appearance and manufacture of this sandal—once to Franciscan monks a symbol of poverty—have changed little over the centuries. Sturdy with natural or brown leather and a sole that is meant to last a long time, it is a sandal that is hard to wear out, except perhaps when on a pilgrimage. Giving it glamour is next to impossible, even when worn with white ankle socks by Chloë Sevigny at the Coachella Valley Music and Arts Festival in California—which is saying something! A staid sandal if there ever was one, it is worn willingly on Paris's Left Bank, however, and along France's Atlantic shore, which is ever so much more chic than the garish Riviera.

TOTAL COMFORT

French women, who have long been devoted to style over comfort, first looked down on the Birkenstock with its unpronounceable name and quasi-orthopedic aspect, although it is much liked by German tourists. It was worn in the Vietnam War era by protesting students on American campuses, but French women only started wearing it without blushing in the 1990s. Who could have imagined that so clunky a sandal would in a few years become a fashionable shoe worn by nearly all the Hollywood stars and most of Paris's trendsetters? In France you'll find it in colors that do not exist anywhere else, as the brand has evolved from its Germanic origins to the Saint Germain-des-Prés aesthetic.

Know that French women prefer to wear the Birkenstock barefoot, their toenails painted flashily, playing against any potential Girl Scout misconception by pairing it with a sophisticated outfit. In 2013, the designer Phoebe Philo made a mink-lined Birkenstock, setting off the retro craze for this all-terrain sandal. J. Crew and Alexander Wang have also drawn inspiration from the Birkenstock, which has a strong reputation for comfort and durability. Even Garance Doré, the French fashion blogger, has been seduced by them and posted a picture of herself on Instagram wearing them with socks! If you find genuine Birkenstocks dull, you can always treat yourself to the revamped stiletto-heeled version by Stella McCartney. It's got it all: the cork sole, the famous buckle, and a spike heel!

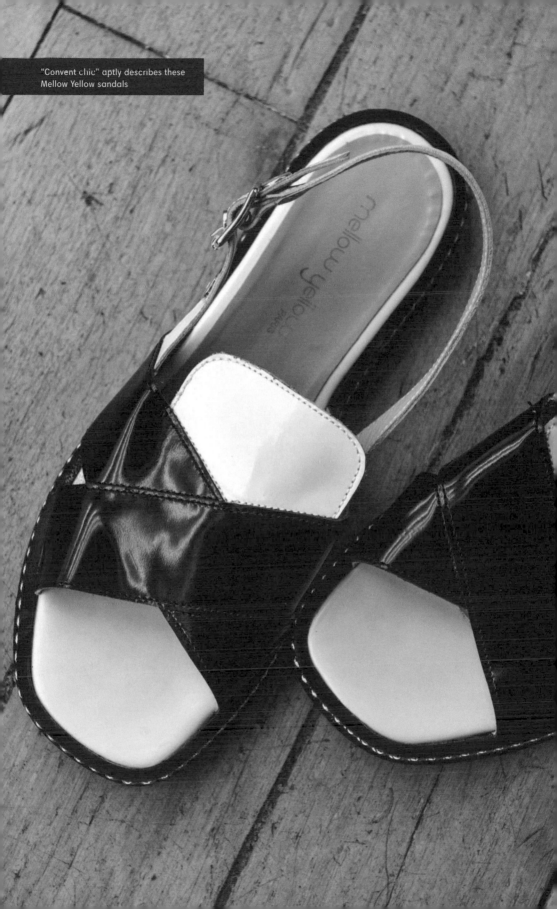

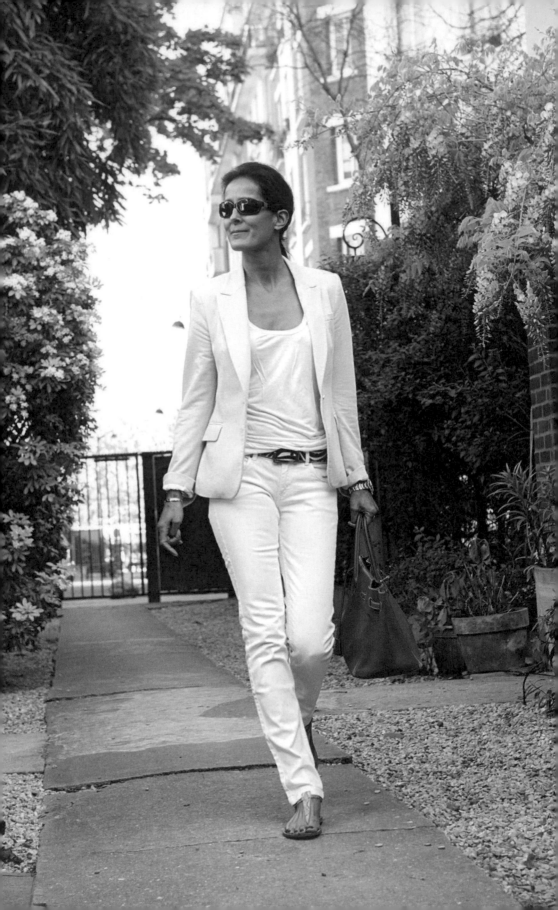

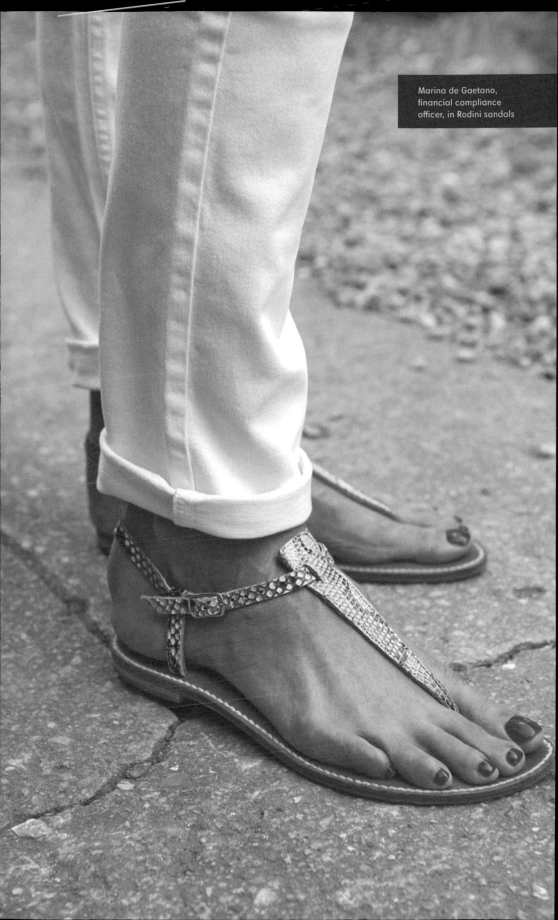

Marina de Gaetano,
financial compliance
officer, in Rodini sandals

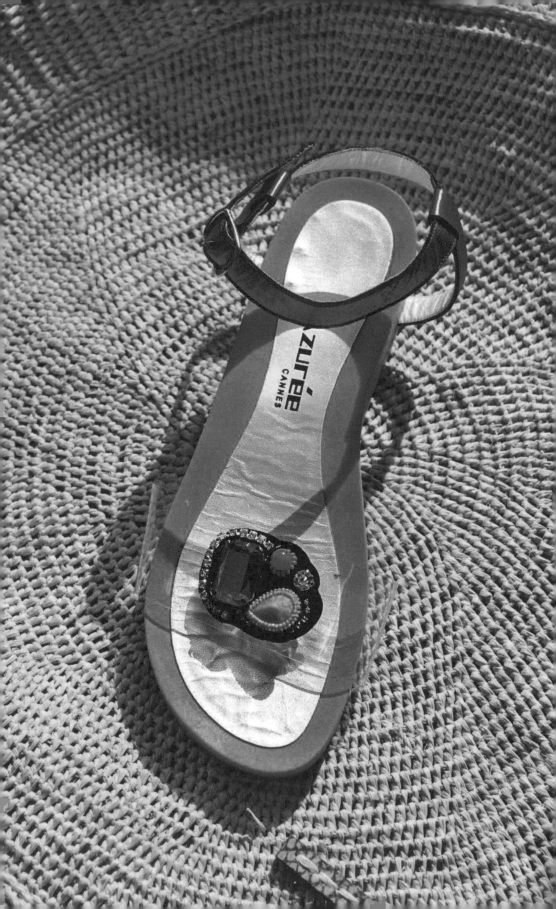

Opposite: The foot is held by a wide, transparent strap in these Cristal sandals by Azurée, a French company that still manufactures in Cannes.

JELLIES

As children, we went clam digging, our feet protected by cheap but effective jelly sandals. This famous beach shoe was developed in the Puy-de-Dôme region in 1946, where it was originally known as the "Sarraizienne." Made of flexible plastic with a tough, anti-skid sole, it was first used as a laborer's shoe in French West Africa. In the 1960s, French vacationers adopted it for trips to the beach. Today, more than one hundred million pairs have been sold for clambering over rocks!

In 2003, the Humeau-Beaupréau company bought the production facilities for the Sarraizienne, copyrighted the French name for jelly sandals, "medusa," and has since produced five hundred thousand pairs a year. This little beach sandal has even bewitched some red carpet regulars. Anne Hathaway and Elle Fanning have been spotted with pale pink jellies on their feet!

But the big winner in plastic sandals has been the Brazilian brand Melissa. Taking inspiration from French jellies, the company created the Aranha in 1979, which has had worldwide success with its ballet flats, sandals, and pumps made of recycled PVC and designed by famous names like Vivienne Westwood and Jason Wu.

With plastic no longer just for those on all-inclusive vacations, even the hipper luxury brands started experimenting: pastel colors and spangles at Topshop, low heels at Givenchy. The Brazilian company iPanema, famous for its flip-flops, has extended its range to every sort of plastic sandal.

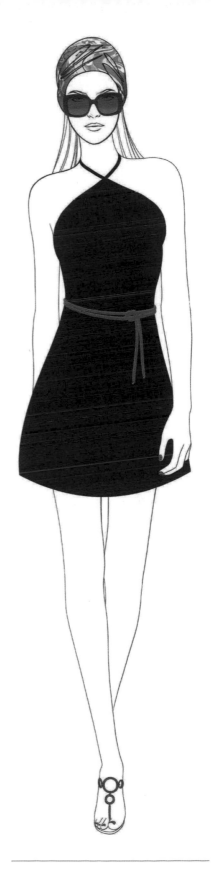

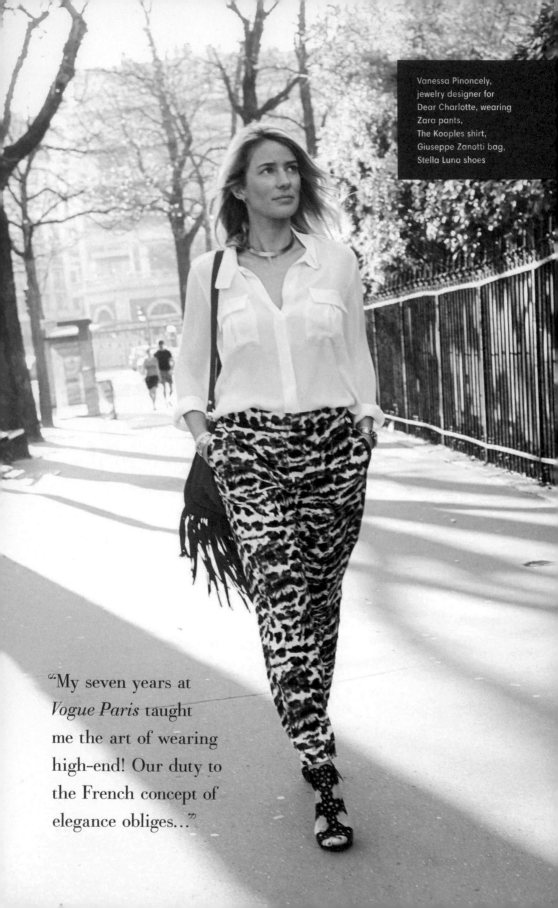

Vanessa Pinoncely,
jewelry designer for
Dear Charlotte, wearing
Zara pants,
The Kooples shirt,
Giuseppe Zanotti bag,
Stella Luna shoes

"My seven years at
Vogue Paris taught
me the art of wearing
high-end! Our duty to
the French concept of
elegance obliges…"

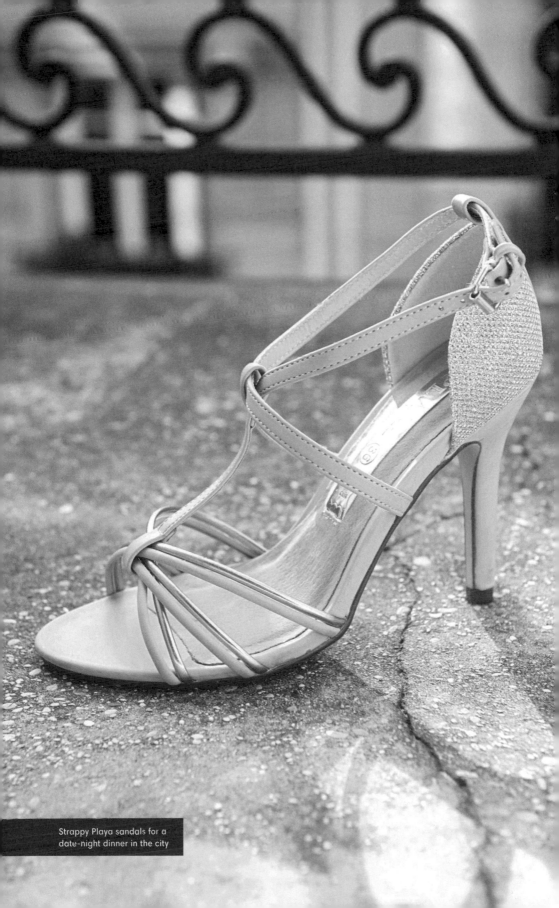

Strappy Playa sandals for a
date-night dinner in the city

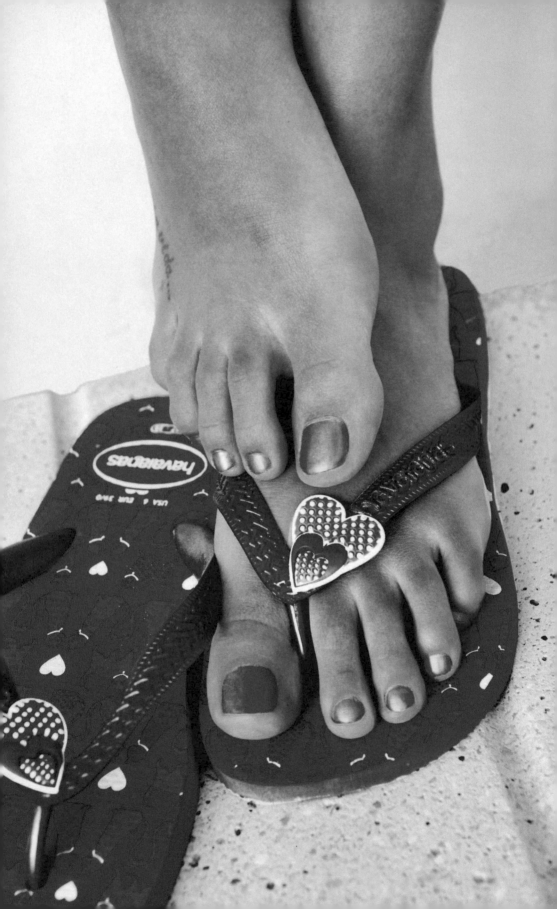

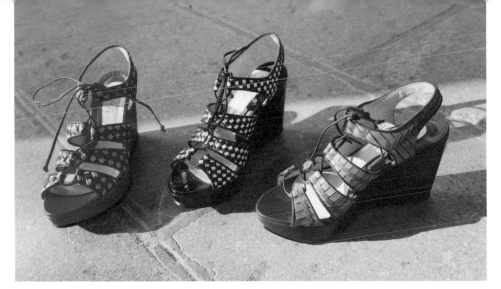

Delage platform sandals

SAY NO TO FLIP-FLOPS!

Did you know that wearing thongs or flip-flops can damage your feet and put strain on your whole body? Unsupported, your feet work harder, which in the long run wears out your tendons and deforms your toes as they are forced to contract to grip the thong. Your arch can also be damaged. With your feet too flat, your whole skeleton has to compensate, from heel to ankle, and on up the spine. There are places where having waterproof sandals is an advantage, but once off the beach and back in town, we put our flip-flops away. They have no more elegance than pool slides + socks à la Mark Zuckerberg. And if you must, for comfort, choose thongs with a heel strap, so that they stay on better. Also keep in mind that a pair of flip-flops can harbor more than eighteen thousand kinds of bacteria! Remember to wash them regularly, especially if they're made of plastic. And replace them often!

Opposite:
Havaianas flip-flops are
better at the beach!

A Very Short Anatomy Lesson

· · · · · · · · · · · · · · · ·

Your foot consists of twenty-six bones, twenty muscles, and thirty-three joints.

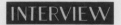

Walter Steiger

DIRECTOR OF LA MAISON

· · · · · · · · · · · · · · · · · ·

The inventor of the ultra-sexy, cult-favorite Curved Heel makes shoes for the most elegant women on the planet. He can also grab our attention with his flats.

Which type of shoes are your favorite to design?

Although I create shoes with a relaxed look as well as other, more sexy ones—high heels with double platforms, for instance—I admit that I derive more pleasure from making heels. My flat patent leather pump, Smoking, was first based on a man's formal shoe and created several seasons ago. After repeated requests, I brought it out in a women's version. I redesigned it with a rubber sole. This shoe has now been around for years and is one of our most popular items.

In your opinion, where does our addictive passion for shoes come from?

Shoes modify the way you walk, etherealize the leg, and make you more attractive and sexy in the eyes of men. This fascination makes shoes an essential item of seduction. But elegance is not what you wear; it's how you wear it! It's very clear that if you can handle high heels with elegance, it makes things even better! People often say, "The higher, the sexier," but it's also your walk that makes you sexy or not!

How does Victoria Beckham manage to walk in your five-inch heels, looking very comfortable and carrying her little girl in her arms?

The secret… her boots are built with an arched footbed and a platform. The whole thing has been worked out so that a woman can walk all day in them. Victoria Beckham bought them at Barneys, and it's surely from having worn them that she asked her right-hand man to contact us to start a collaboration.

You have a real fan club…

Every time I visit New York, I go to my Park Avenue store and I very often encounter one of my faithful clients. I think she has been buying my shoes since the beginning, back in the 1970s. She always buys the strongest designs in the collection. In fact, I think she knows my collections better than I do! I'm proud to think that despite all the years I've been at it, my sense of style has survived.

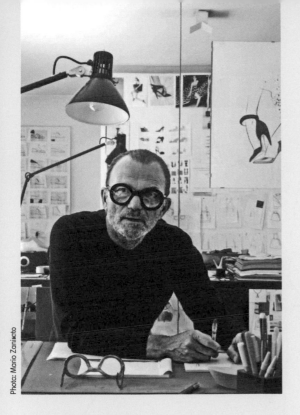

Photo: Mario Zaniexto

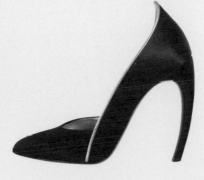

The famous Curved Heel

Is there such a thing as a shoe that looks good on every woman?

I'd be tempted to say no, because each woman is unique and has her own style, her own temperament; although in the past few seasons, sneakers seem to be everywhere and they adapt to every different shape of foot.

How has women's taste changed in the past ten or twenty years?

It's quite strange… fashion is more and more highly specialized. And a parallel development is that people follow fashion less.

Does the "French touch" still exist? Do French women have a particular taste in shoes?

I came to Paris for the first time when I was twenty, because for me Paris was the capital of fashion. And fifty years later, Paris remains and will continue to remain, I hope, the most creative place for fashion. Most trends still start in Paris, even if other cities contribute. But for me, the Parisian woman is still *the* example of style.

"Elegance is not what you wear; it's how you wear it!"

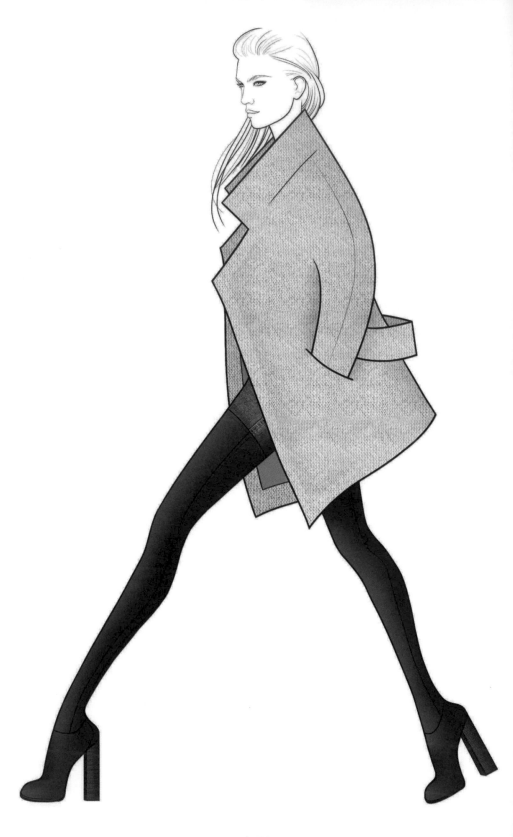

THE ONES WE LOVE TO HATE

· · · · · · · · · · · · · · · · ·

Some women love them. Others swear they'll never wear them. And others still—often the same—end up wearing them anyway. A woman will sometimes change her mind. All the better. The shoes in this chapter are tricky to wear, but these shoes with a bad reputation may well capture your fancy. The important thing is to choose carefully and wear them well.

THIGH-HIGH BOOTS

No. Equipped with tall, slender heels, thigh-high boots have a way of teleporting you into the middle of a remake of *Pretty Woman*, where that lady-of-loose-morals label hangs in the air. Flat-heeled and flaring at the knee, they might help you seduce Robin Hood; Puss in Boots is also a possibility. Pointy, with stretch fabric soles, they authorize you to straddle a motorcycle... made of plastic—the bad-girl look falls flat. And when you talk about over-the-knee boots, you'd better have skinny legs. Bluntly, this undemocratic footwear makes no allowances for squishy thighs, fat calves, or legs like posts.

Yes. We like the very feminine ones of soft leather or kid that sheath your leg like a second skin. The prettiest are the ones constantly being reissued by Chanel, Alaïa, and Isabel Marant. Yes, you have to earn your thigh-highs.

You wear them soberly. Certainly not with pants (where is your harmonica?), nor with a flounced dress (where are your pigtails?), but with a slightly austere above-the-knee tunic dress.

COWBOY BOOTS

No. Yee-haw! Cowboy boots with four-inch heels regularly try to infiltrate our closets. Stay away, especially when paired with cowboy apparel—leave out the cowboy shirt and oversized pair of faded jeans.

Yes. Why not, if you wear them with elegance? (But that's rarely the case.) We prefer the original ones: topstitching, a toe that curves up a little, and a heel that is a bit but not too sharply angled. And try to revisit the cowboy ethos on a more urban note—pair the boots with clothes more in sync with *Sex and the City* than *Once Upon a Time in the West.*

Many versions of the cowboy boot exist that have taken inspiration from the original but are easier to live with: The tall Western shaft has been cut down to ankle-boot height, the wooden heel is straighter and the toe more rounded. Our favorite: those by Mexicana. Or the famous Dicker by Isabel Marant, copied a thousand times but never matched. Reimagined in this way, cowboy boots lend themselves to various sartorial games. Worn with a wide-legged pair of jeans, they can evoke Marilyn Monroe in *The Misfits,* or they can give a little backbone to a frilly, romantic dress, pep up a pair of colored or patterned pants, and in the summertime give a suggestive kick to cut-offs or a short skirt.

APRÈS-SKI BOOTS

No. At the foot of the slopes to meet friends around a pot of fondue, Moon Boots have their place. But taken from their proper context it's another story. Is there any point in parading around a major urban center in boots designed for extreme temperatures and deep snow? Are you really that sensitive to cold? Are you really that short on ideas? As to their Australian cousin, the sheepskin UGG, which always looks like footwear for an astronaut, it should be reserved for after surfing or cold snaps. They should never be worn with slouchy clothes. They only accentuate shapelessness.

Yes. For cold snaps and surf parties!

MULES

No. Flat-heeled mules tend to remind us of what the housekeeper wore in old movies. The high-heeled version invites thoughts of bimbos in their boudoirs. You have to be very strict with mules. They should always look box fresh. Toss out any in your collection that have a dowdy spool heel or a pointy toe that is starting to warp upward. Yuck!

Yes. Mules hark back to the pinups of the 1960s. Wear them with a sophisticated outfit that plays on retro nostalgia or forget about them altogether. Try a knee-length pencil skirt and form-fitting pullover à la Dita Von Teese, or a narrow ankle-length pant and a belted shirt, *Mad Men* style. And as long as you're wearing them, walk with a short, definite step.

Opposite:
A flat, silver mule
can also be nice.

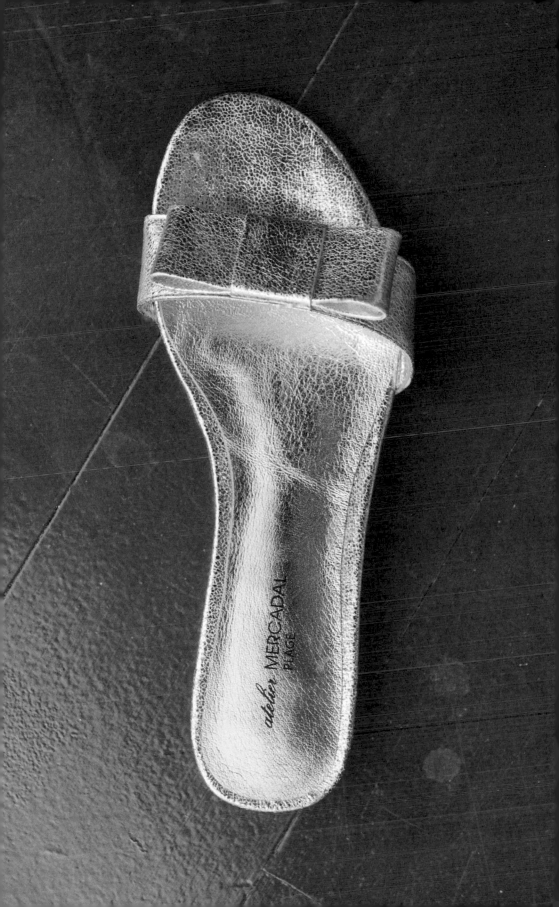

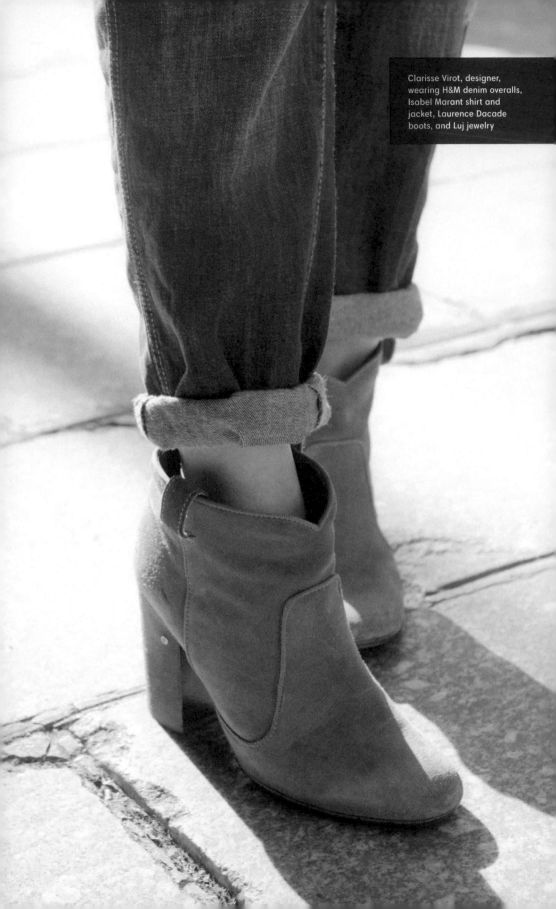

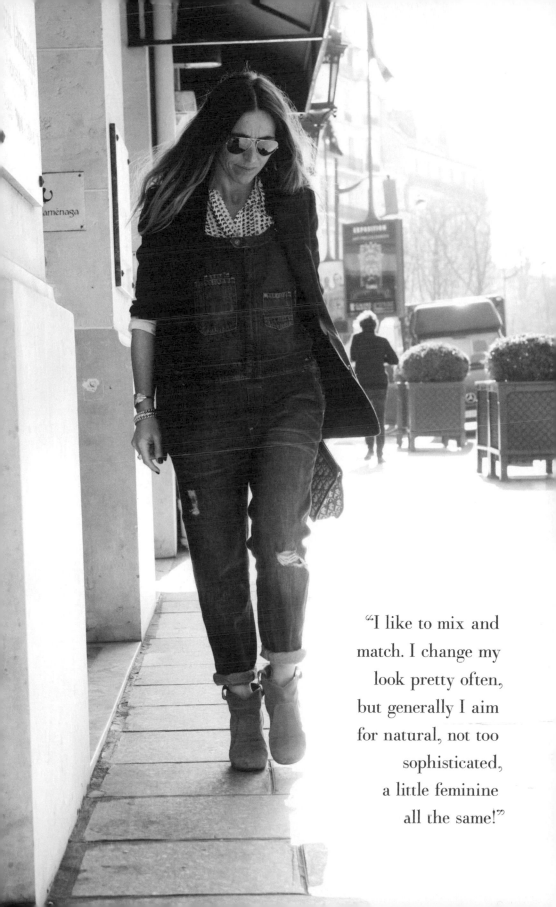

"I like to mix and
match. I change my
look pretty often,
but generally I aim
for natural, not too
sophisticated,
a little feminine
all the same!"

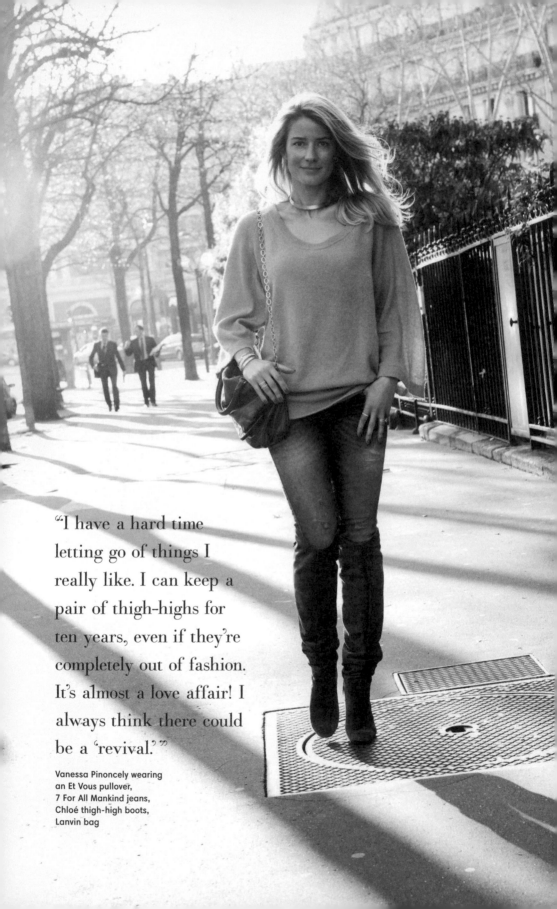

"I have a hard time letting go of things I really like. I can keep a pair of thigh-highs for ten years, even if they're completely out of fashion. It's almost a love affair! I always think there could be a 'revival.'"

Vanessa Pinoncely wearing an Et Vous pullover, 7 For All Mankind jeans, Chloé thigh-high boots, Lanvin bag

CLOGS

No. If the sole doesn't go *clip-clop* when you walk, it's because you're wearing a plastic model. Your profession may authorize you to wear these, particularly if you're in the health sector or the restaurant business. Otherwise, don't let the fashion police catch you wearing them!

Yes. When it comes to clogs, pool slides, and flip-flops, there is only one material for the sole: wood. Different shapes can suggest a nurse, a geisha, or Heidi (a girl of the mountains). We like them all. Despite their rigidity and their weight, wooden sandals are extraordinarily comfortable, made for trotting around all day. More elegant than you might think, they pair well with dresses, skirts, rolled-up chinos, ankle-length pants… You can even wear them in winter— in dry weather—with socks and wool tights. Louboutin himself makes clogs. Our favorites are by Swedish Hasbeens and Kerstin Adolphson.

WEDGES

No. The platform-shoe style puts you right back in the middle of the 1970s. All you need to complete the look is a pair of bell-bottoms. Unless you prefer the wedge sneakers indelibly worn by the Spice Girls in the 1990s. As for wedged pumps, be extra careful to avoid the granny look!

Yes. Wedge heels allow you to gain height while keeping some stability. If they have platforms under the ball of your foot, they give you even more height. Whether boots, ankle boots, or sandals, our preference in wedges is for the lightest and slimmest possible.

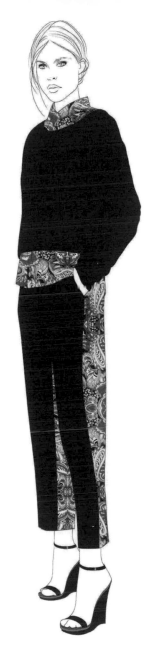

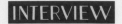

Michel Vivien

ARTIST AND SHOEMAKER

· · · · · · · · · · · · · · · · · ·

Michel Vivien, fascinated by sculpture, designed his first women's shoes when he was only twenty years old, a bit by accident. After collaborating with many fashion houses—Lanvin, Carel, and Charles Jourdan among them—Michel Vivien founded his own business in 1998. Free and independent, he brings together contemporary boldness and a love of traditional craftmanship.

What kind of designer are you?

I create my collections without paying attention to trends. My role is to accompany a woman's walk, marrying elegance, good fit, the curve of the shoe, but also aesthetic rigor and creative spontaneity. My ambition is to make timeless and sensual styles that are untouched by the passing years and seasons. Take the Karluz boot, for example: It was created seven years ago; it's a true weapon of war and seduction on three-and-a-half-inch heels!

Why do women's heels make people fantasize?

Objects of desire, shoes dress a woman's foot and embody her longings for beauty. The shoe is the very real Holy Grail of an entire fantasy of fashion and femininity.

The fact is, when wearing high heels, the few centimeters that separate a woman from the ground and define her silhouette give a certain posture to the shoulders, which project backward. Heels "tense" the silhouette and the body stands straighter. They force a woman to bend, to push her pelvis forward and tense the muscles of her calves. This slight clenching of the calf is sexy.

Feet are the focal point of enormous eroticism. Only a few generations ago, you didn't see women's ankles.

We are inside the male phantasmagoria. In high heels, a woman no longer has the same walk; she advances more slowly; her body sways and undulates. It's only a recent phenomenon to walk in very high heels. That's why, even when I make heels higher than four inches, the curve of the shoe doesn't go beyond a certain height, because a woman's walk would become robotic and ungraceful.

What is true luxury, for you?

The word "luxury" asks to be rethought and is above all a synonym for the rare and exceptional. It breaks free of trends to suggest an

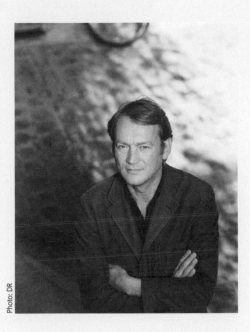

elegance that is recognized and appreciated as a work of art.

Luxury for me is also investment: the hours and hours and hours of exacting and passionate work. There is a real loss of craftmanship. In the last century, the rule was that it took three years to train a worker. Nowadays, three months are considered enough! The great rebirth of luxury will come from quality and know-how. In our day, the luxury of rarity no longer exists. Look at airports: In every city, every country, you see the same chains and the same shops selling products that are duplicated in thousands of copies.

You have a special place among designers of women's shoes. What do women like best: the look or the comfort of your creations?

"Comfort" should be the watchword of the industry. But the word is no longer in fashion. Yet, if I were a pair of women's feet, I would give it enormous importance. Where does a shoe's comfort come from? From the fit, the curvature of the sole, and the rigor it was designed with.

Walking on hard surfaces is a recent thing. Sidewalks and asphalt are terrible for your feet and your back, because there's no shock absorber in shoes. The vibrations are catastrophic for the body. Soles have become very thin compared to the one-inch soles of clogs that most people walked on one hundred years ago. The ground has become an important constraint in the making of a shoe.

The ideal Michel Vivien woman?

The Parisian woman: She has personality, she has breeding, her elegance is simple, she expresses her femininity with infinite naturalness. And I hope my game is strong enough to attract both mother and daughter!

BOOTS MADE FOR WALKING (AND MORE!)

Women were forbidden to wear boots before the French Revolution, but they have made up for lost time since then! Boots are now one of the sexiest, most provocative items of feminine attire.

Formerly reserved for soldiers and equestrians, boots first surfaced in women's fashion in the 1960s along with the miniskirt, a symbol of feminine freedom and rebellion. Twiggy, Emma Peel, and Barbarella, who all embraced the boot trend, embodied a powerful, seductive, and uncomplicated femininity.

When Brigitte Bardot appeared in thigh-highs, the French troubadour Serge Gainsbourg was moved to write a song in her praise.

The riding boot canonized by Hermès is still a popular item today, but it is generally worn a long way from the stables. With heels of varying heights, boots, mid-calf boots, ankle boots, and other booties can be seen on women's feet at school gates, cocktail parties, and formal dinners on every day of the week from dawn to dusk and from dusk to dawn, in fair weather and foul. Made of leather, lace, or rubber, they have become style staples, whether worn with a dress, a skirt, shorts, or pants, wearable in summer and winter alike.

WHICH BOOTS ARE BEST?

How can you make do with only one pair? For our part, if we had to choose just one, we'd settle for the straight-shafted cowboy-style roper called the Camarguaise. While they can fit neatly under the legs of your jeans, they can also give an edge to a sweet, bucolic dress or tame the fire of a short skirt.

This is similar to what motorcycle boots can do, which is make anything look unstuffy.

Others prefer the more classic and discreet look of riding boots or the female-executive connotations of high-heeled black boots for their forays into almost any territory. And some day we dream of having outrageous high-heel stripper boots loaded with sex appeal and made of lambskin so glove-like that it clings to the curve of your calves like a second skin.

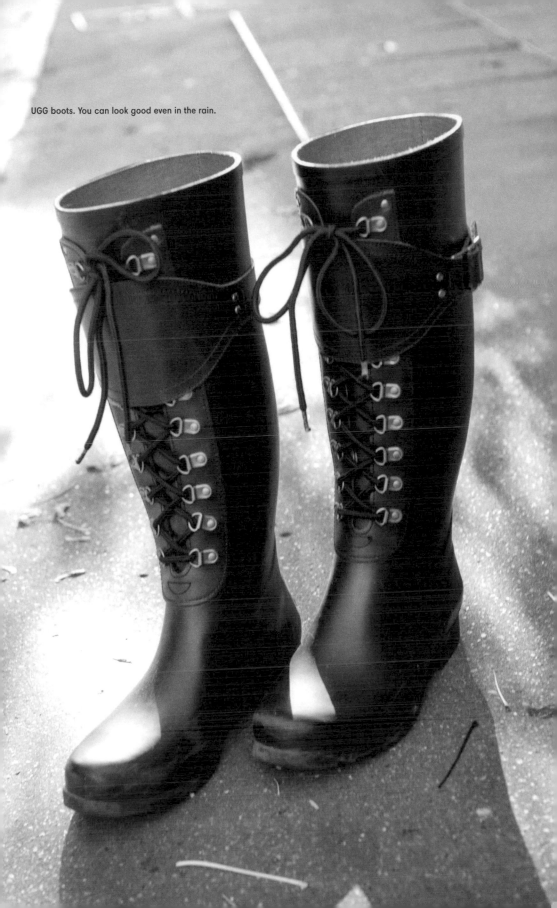
UGG boots. You can look good even in the rain.

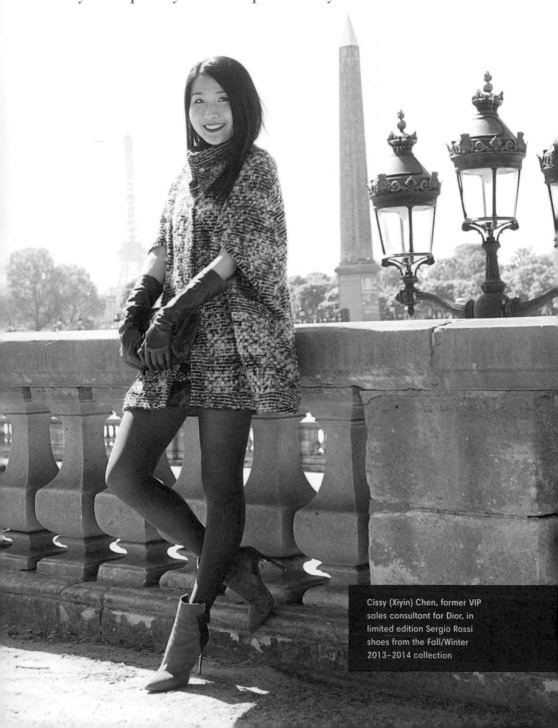

"I learned in Paris the importance of accessories.
A striking pair of heels can transform a basic outfit
[white t-shirt + skinny jeans/black leggings] into
something very chic. That's maybe why I love shoes,
they can quickly define a personality."

Cissy (Xiyin) Chen, former VIP
sales consultant for Dior, in
limited edition Sergio Rossi
shoes from the Fall/Winter
2013–2014 collection

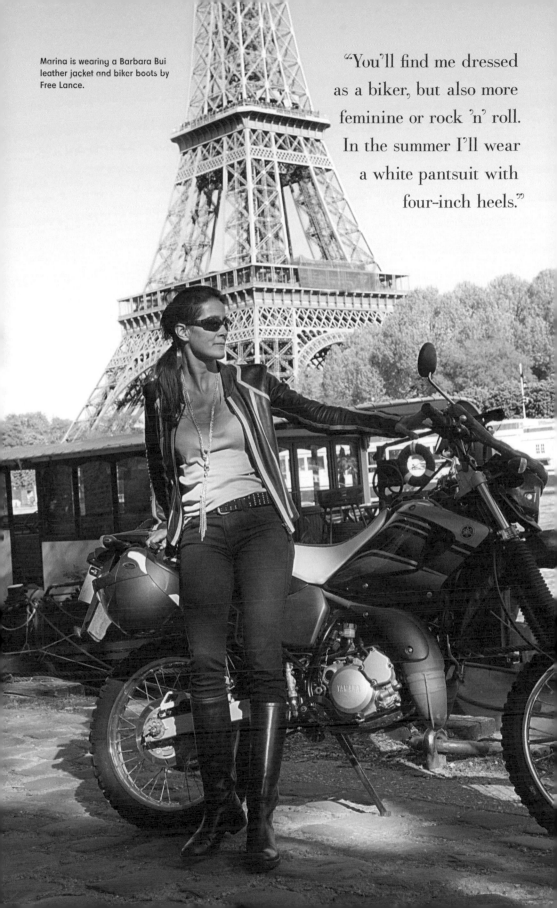

Marina is wearing a Barbara Bui leather jacket and biker boots by Free Lance.

"You'll find me dressed as a biker, but also more feminine or rock 'n' roll. In the summer I'll wear a white pantsuit with four-inch heels."

FRENCH ROPERS

La Botte Gardiane, a company that has made shoes since the 1950s, was bought by the Agulhon family in 1995. These two brothers and their sister are passionate about shoes and have modernized the traditional models, including the boots worn by the *gardians* (French cowboys), while staying faithful to French craftsmanship and production methods. This new, modern style of the classic cowboy boot has been dubbed *roper* after the calf-ropers in a rodeo. The shoes have attracted attention abroad, in Japan in particular, and the boots are carried in some of the trendiest stores in France.

AIGLE BOOTS

This very French company was created by Hiram Hutchinson, an American who lived in France. He chose the name Aigle, which means *eagle*, in homage to the national emblem of the United States.

Although first worn for farming, then for sports and leisure activities like riding and sailing, Aigle boots are now seen regularly on the streets of Paris. It is not uncommon to find beautiful, hip young women wearing these colorful rubber boots on their feet and trendy bags over their shoulders.

UGGS, THE CRAZE FROM AUSTRALIA

Watching them sag and melt around their owners' ankles like an ice cream in the sun, you know that at least podiatrists and physical therapists will still have work in the years ahead! Invented by Australian surfer Shane Stedman to warm surfers' feet after a session catching icy waves, this shapeless boot quickly became a trendy item in Hollywood and beyond. This boot's success has us asking ourselves a philosophical question, namely: Does comfort take precedence over aesthetics?

If you like UGGs (you're allowed to), try not to pair them with an orange tan, a bad blow-dry, a glitzy manicure, or overly tight jeans. Go for a healthy, California look with naturally sun-streaked hair, frayed blue-jean shorts, and a tanned and muscled leg. In our opinion as slightly uptight French women, UGGs don't work so well in the city.

THE TWO COMMANDMENTS FOR PURCHASING BOOTS

In our latitudes, boots and ankle boots are worn for several months of the year. They are generally an important purchase and also a considerable investment.

Can You Wear Boots with Bare Legs?

Ever since Kate Moss showed us how cool it was to revel in shorts and rubber boots at the Glastonbury Festival, we have dared to wear boots without tights. Yes, it's possible. But only when you're going casual—ropers and shorts—and not so much with a tailored skirt and office boots.

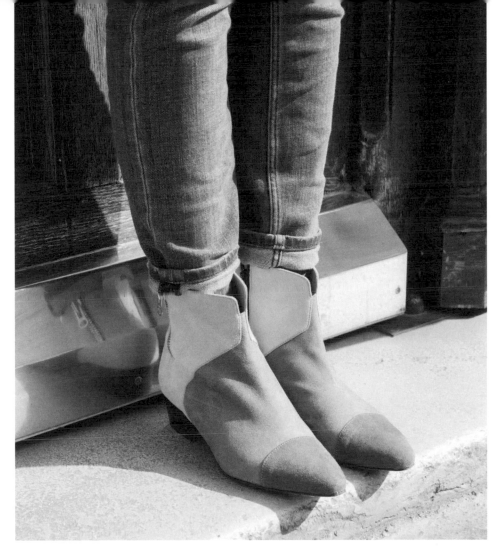
Heimstone booties

First commandment: Thou shalt choose quality. Forget about split leather, reconstituted leather, "suede-like" stretch fabrics, and that nasty lining of synthetic fur. Opt for calfskin or lined leather. With quality comes durability and comfort.

Second commandment: Thou shalt choose the right size. More than any other shoe, boots have a way of telling you if you've got the wrong size. No, a boot won't "adapt to your feet." Try on boots in the evening, because after an active day, your feet will have swollen slightly and you'll be more likely to buy the right size. And don't forget to think about the thickness of the socks you'll be wearing when the weather turns cold.

We give high marks for comfort and quality to La Botte Gardiane, Sartore, Free Lance, Mexicana, Chie Mihara, Frye, and Laurence Dacade.

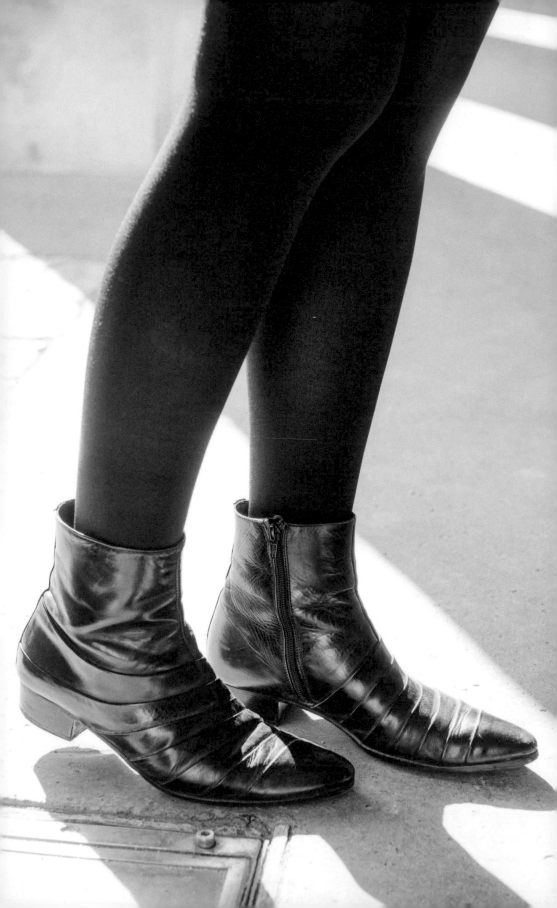

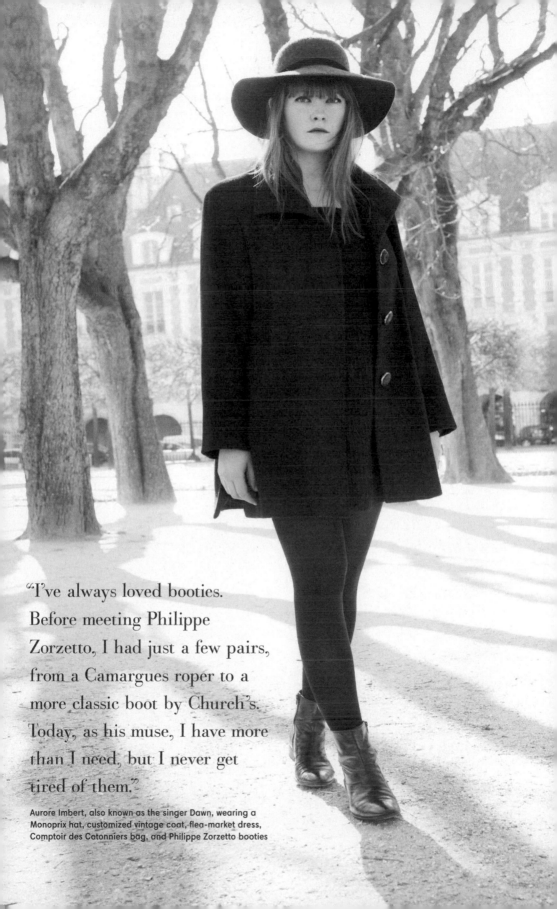

"I've always loved booties. Before meeting Philippe Zorzetto, I had just a few pairs, from a Camargues roper to a more classic boot by Church's. Today, as his muse, I have more than I need, but I never get tired of them."

Aurore Imbert, also known as the singer Dawn, wearing a Monoprix hat, customized vintage coat, flea-market dress, Comptoir des Cotonniers bag, and Philippe Zorzetto booties

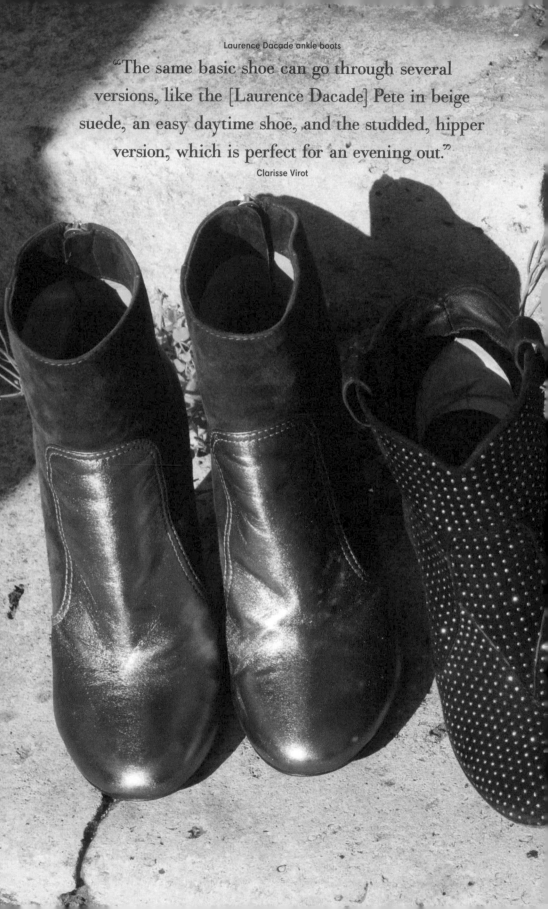

Laurence Dacade ankle boots

"The same basic shoe can go through several versions, like the [Laurence Dacade] Pete in beige suede, an easy daytime shoe, and the studded, hipper version, which is perfect for an evening out."

Clarisse Virot

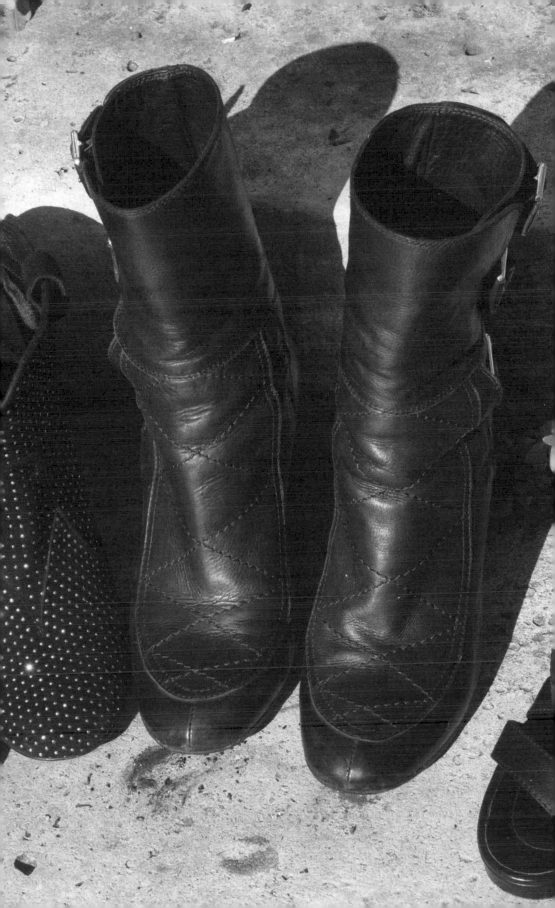

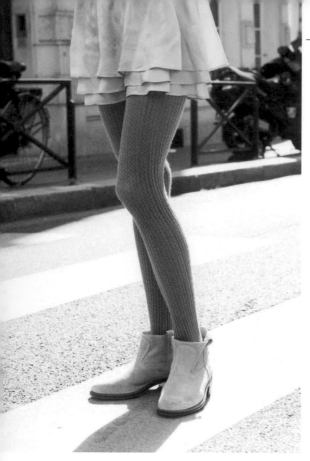

We give high marks
for comfort and quality
to La Botte Gardiane,
Sartore, Free Lance,
Mexicana, Chie Mihara,
Frye, and Laurence
Dacade.

A mix of things:
Dim pantyhose,
La Botte Gardiane booties,
and a satin skirt

HOW SHOULD YOU CHOOSE BOOTS AND ANKLE BOOTS?

➡ Unless you are slender and long-limbed, always show a little skin to slim your figure. For instance, avoid wearing a boot that comes right to the height of a knee-length skirt. Wear an ankle boot instead; it's more modern.

➡ If you have heavy calves, forget stretch boots that compress your legs. Even if you manage to slide your gams into them, they'll bunch up in a way that isn't nice. Instead, go for slightly flaring boots of soft leather or nubuck. And if your legs are sturdy, stay away from booties that stop at ankle height.

➡ If you're short, avoid boots that rise to just below the calf. They may make you look shorter. Instead, wear ankle boots or mid-calf boots with medium-high heels.

➡ If your calves are very slender, beware of riding boots made to fit the curve of a calf much larger than your own. Choose tall, straight boots instead, and if you're on the tall side, consider calfskin thigh-highs or booties.

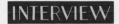

Antoine Agulhon

MAKER OF CAMARGUAISE (FRENCH COWBOY) BOOTS

• • • • • • • • • • • • • • • • • •

La Botte Gardiane is a classically French company, established in 1958. After changing hands in 1995, it became a family-owned business. We asked a few questions of Antoine Agulhon, a co-director of the company.

What do you answer when people say your boots are expensive?

We use full-grain leather, which is more complicated to work with. For the lining, we use calfskin, which is stronger than pigskin but costs twice as much. After you've worn a pair of shoes for a year, you'll see the difference. For our Camargues boots, we use a thicker and stronger leather, but one that's harder to work with. About 95 percent of manufacturers use thin leather, lined with pigskin, rather than a good, thick leather. But two pieces of thin leather will never be as long lasting as one piece of good, thick leather. People like this quality, and we export to every part of the world. We target a high-end market, one that is specialized and exacting—a clientele of connoisseurs who are looking for the made-in-France craftmanship, and who respond to the fact that we have our own ateliers. Our manufacturing is done 100 percent at our workshop in Villetelle (between Nîmes and Montpellier).

We also train our workers; they are the ones who have the know-how. When a factory shuts down, you lose that know-how. People who can assemble shoes are growing scarce.

Why have you chosen to manufacture your product in France?

Because we control the production and it's an assurance of quality. Everything is done in the workshop: cutting, assembly, and finishing. It costs more, unquestionably, but it cuts down on production time, and we can react more quickly than if we sub-contracted. It allows us to manufacture in small batches. The cutting station, which is a key process, benefits from our attention, which wouldn't happen if we manufactured outside of France.

My workers are not paid on a volume or a piecework basis, unlike in many countries. We reward quality and the time that is put into something. I've had the chance to see factories where the workers are paid for their output, and it changes your outlook toward the work.

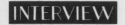

Anne Tourneux

STYLIST FOR TELEVISION

· · · · · · · · · · · · · · · · ·

"The shoes you need to have: boots and classic black pumps—timeless, with a beautiful cut. Do not hesitate to go to major brands (Jimmy Choo, Prada, Saint Laurent…). They will accompany you everywhere for years, just like a nice blazer and a good pair of jeans."

Do you remember your first "good" pair of shoes?

I quickly became enamored with pretty shoes, and I learned how to tell the difference early on by accompanying my mother into shoe shops as a child. Already then I knew how to choose. I bought my first truly good pair of shoes when I was seventeen, a pair of cowboy boots—the Jean Paul Gaultier era—with laces. They were spectacular. Afterwards it became a ritual, when I started to work. I would systematically buy myself designer shoes. My wardrobe was composed of simple clothes, but when it came to shoes, I rejected all compromise. If I'd kept everything, I'd have a museum! I gave lots of pairs away to friends over the years.

What are the shoes that you use most often?

On a daily basis, by far and away it would be slip-on boots. I adore ankle boots and I collect them. What I like now is a shoe that doesn't cause me discomfort but that doesn't cut back on style. I'm addicted to agnès b.'s Rock n Roll slip-on boots, a staple of my collection, which I'll probably buy in every color.

At night or for a special get-together, I like to wear black pumps. I have some in every heel height. My favorites are python-skin Pradas, classic and truly elegant. I wear mid-heels on a normal day, but, if I could, I would wear high heels every day. There's no other sensation like it: You feel more feminine, more confident in heels.

How much suffering will you accept for your shoes?

I used to accept a lot [*laughs*]. And I had some very painful experiences. I don't do that anymore. I even go so far as to buy a size larger than my foot so that I can add an insole or comfortable padding.

Do you have "enough" shoes?

When you're in love, you don't count! I never have enough; every season presents me with new temptations. But the act of waiting and not giving in to impulse (to which I largely succumbed at the start) allows me to buy myself *the* pair of shoes that I am going to keep preciously. I installed wall cabinets in my entryway so that I'd have a place for them all. I often open them to bring out a shoe that I'll put on show somewhere in the house so I can see it, because I wear slip-on boots three-quarters of the time. I love bringing out the oldest shoes I've kept. It truly brings me face-to-face with my identity.

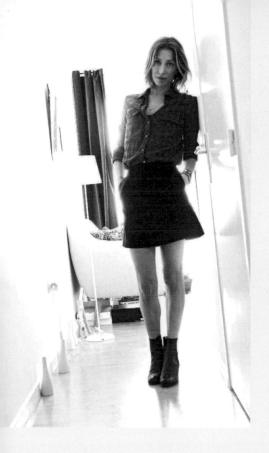

Anne Tourneux wearing a Zadig & Voltaire shirt, Acne skirt, agnès b. shoes, bracelet by Chan Luu, necklace and earrings by Vanrycke

But you can tell a nice shoe from the quality of its materials (leather interior, leather sole, surface coating…) and the delicacy of its shape, the finishing touches, and the curve, of course. This alchemy is especially practiced among designers, and naturally it comes at a price.

Are there fashion no-nos? What should you never wear?

If there's a no-no, it's wearing very high shoes of very low quality. It destroys any idea of chic. I would always opt for a very beautiful pair of heels over five pairs made of imitation leather.

What's the worst mistake you've made?

I freely admit all my mistakes in this area, and there have been many! There was a long time when I was drawn to experimental shoes. I saw them as performances: Tabi slip-ons by Margiela, ankle boots of vegetable-tanned leather with wood and metal heels by Stella McCartney, Spikes by Louboutin. The odder it was, the more I was intrigued by it. Today I'm much wiser in my choices, but I still look at a shoe's eccentricity the way you might look at a performance. Phoebe Philo's shoes for Céline are some of the most thought-provoking.

What shoes do you want to get next?

Suede pumps with slender heels, ankle boots (again) like the ones by Laurence Dacade, the Célines with metal heels from last winter, or the mythic shoes that I missed out on their first time around, like the Cage shoes by Saint Laurent, which someday I'll track down on the Internet.

What are your criteria for buying a pair of shoes?

It's quite subjective and personal, but if you're not going to be led astray you have to think about the intended use of the shoe. Your shoes can be thought of along the same lines as your wardrobe: You need the basics (black pumps, ankle boots, sandals, evening shoes…) and some more personal and intuitive choices to liven up your silhouette (colors, heels, shapes). Today we have a very wide array of choices; there is a wealth of options in every price range. But I still can't bring myself to buy a shoe that doesn't have a leather sole and a leather interior. But I say that having just bought for the first time a satin kitten-heel shoe from Zara, so tempting with its mini-heel… You can really talk yourself into almost anything when you become fixated on a design.

NOT WITHOUT MY PUMPS!
YES, BUT WHICH ONES?

....

What would we do without them? They are with us at our office parties, our moments of celebration, our formal and improvised evening engagements. They also come to our rescue on days when we don't want to dress up at all. They have a way of injecting a little chic into the lazy woman's duo of slim jeans and t-shirt, and they bring the right amount of femininity to a slouchy pant. Don't buy the wrong ones!

Pumps are in every woman's clothes closet, and they are also the ancestors of practically all our shoes. Derived from a man's shoe—originally without heels or straps—they were adopted by women toward the middle of the eighteenth century. A French aristocrat—Alfred-Guillaume-Gabriel, Count d'Orsay—gave them their original profile, which would survive a succession of revolutions, fashions, moods, and eras!

They are worn high-heeled or low, variably open, and made of leather, sharkskin, silk, satin, or just about any other material you can imagine. They can be two-colored, pointed, square-toed, jeweled, plain; the list goes on…

HOW SHOULD YOU CHOOSE THEM?

You want them with only a slightly pointed toe. The days of super-pointy pumps are long gone.

You want them to be the right height, which is to say not too short. And the right height is simply the height that doesn't curb your freedom of movement. At what level you top out—whether two inches or five—is up to you.

You want them low cut. If you have a pretty foot, the lower the better.

You want them to be sober and elegant (Gabrielle 2, by Charles Jourdan), with a platform (Sledge, by L.K.Bennett), metallic gold (Katar by Patricia Blanchet), sensually curved (Titine by Fred Marzo), in red patent leather (Amélie by François Najar), peep-toed with python uppers (Eva by François Najar), made of cork (Audrey by Amélie Pichard), two-toned (Marisa by Atelier Mercadal), with pop art motifs (Fibule by Jancovek), sporting the British flag (Duranduran by Annabel Winship) or stars (Nadine by Annabel Winship)… We are ready to bet that you can add more to this wish list.

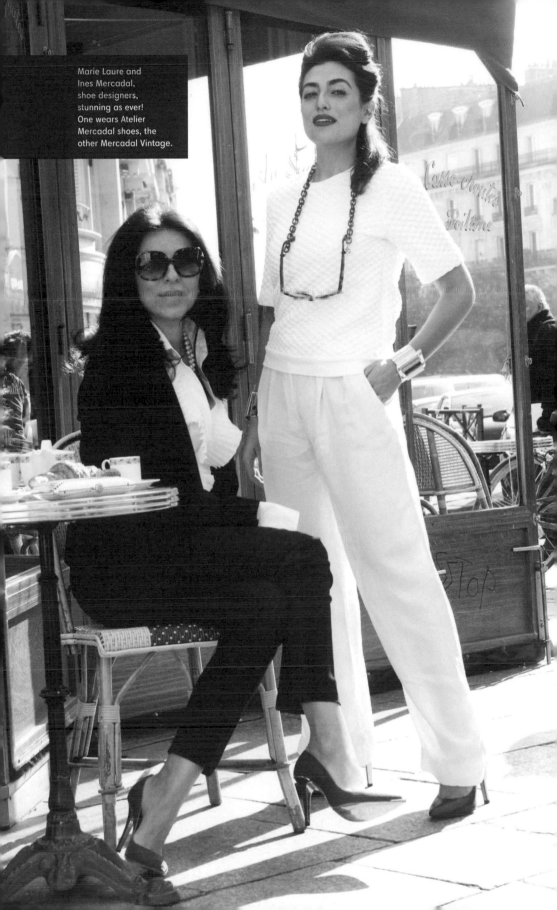

Marie Laure and
Ines Mercadal,
shoe designers,
stunning as ever!
One wears Atelier
Mercadal shoes, the
other Mercadal Vintage.

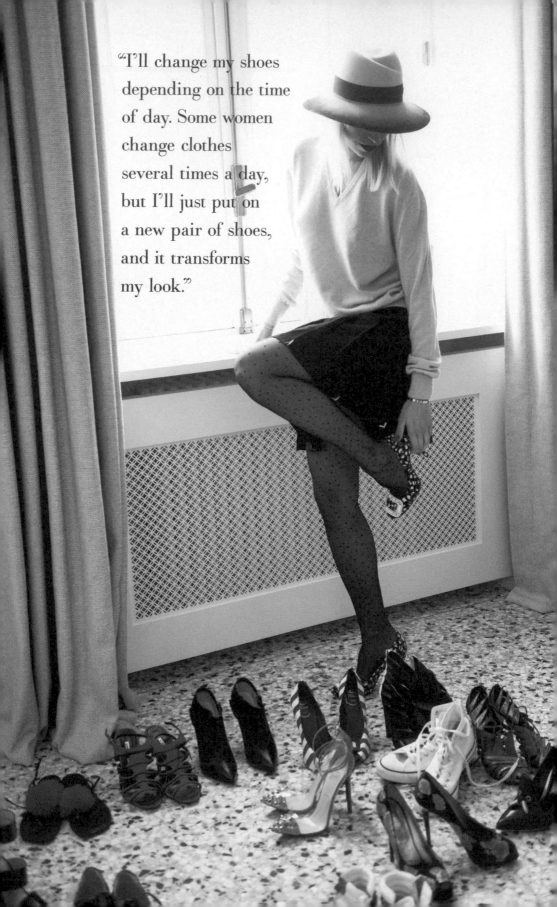

"I'll change my shoes depending on the time of day. Some women change clothes several times a day, but I'll just put on a new pair of shoes, and it transforms my look."

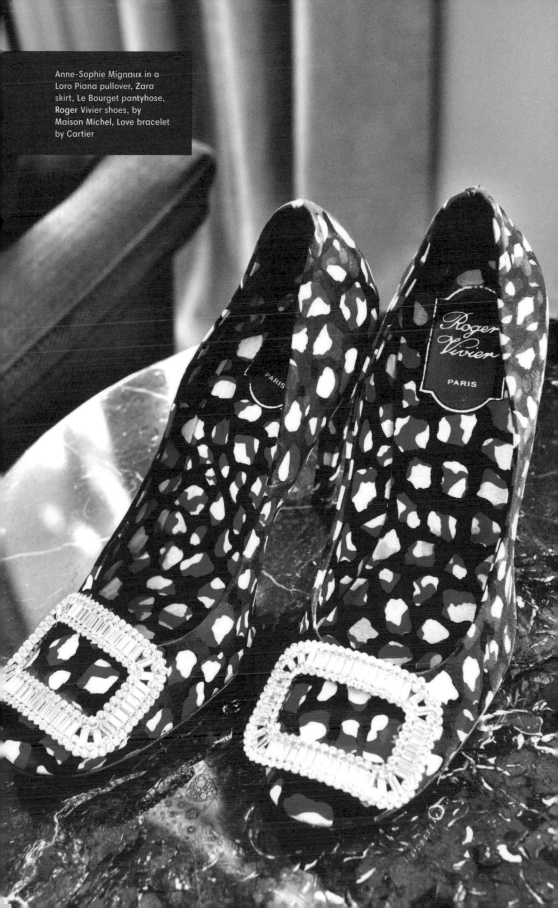

Anne-Sophie Mignaux in a
Loro Piana pullover, Zara
skirt, Le Bourget pantyhose,
Roger Vivier shoes, by
Maison Michel, Love bracelet
by Cartier

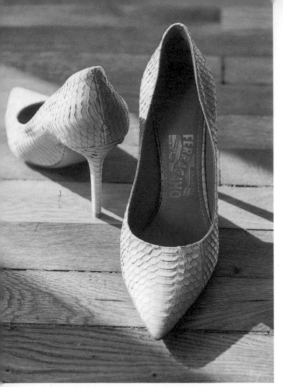

Python-skin pumps by Salvatore Ferragamo

MUST YOU ABSOLUTELY OWN A PAIR OF BLACK PUMPS?

Using the little-black-dress argument, people have told us that it's only right to own a pair of black pumps. But in fact, this great classic is not a staple for everyone. Some women prefer oxfords or slip-ons or red patent leather pumps. While it's true that black pumps work well with office clothes or a tiny evening outfit, they sometimes lack dynamism and a sense of fun—especially when worn on legs that haven't seen the sun in months. Less severe than patent leather is black suede, along the lines of Isabel Marant's Poppy, the symbol of easy Parisian chic.

Don't be afraid of colors, different materials, or a combination of the two. If you're wearing a printed fabric, choose shoes matching one of the colors in it. Take a chance on contrasts and try complementary colors, which will mutually enhance each other. For instance, pick a luminous blue to go with a nice orange outfit.

If you're determined to have black pumps, select a handsome leather, a trustworthy supplier, and a beautiful line. For evening wear, avoid low, square heels, which make you look heavier, and high-cut styles that cover your foot, making you look older. And choose lightweight pantyhose (20 deniers), lace or satin-stitch tights, or a pretty seamed stocking.

CAN YOU WEAR ANKLE SOCKS WITH PUMPS?

It's a matter of taste. We have met partisans who embrace this style in every age group, and we have met dyed-in-the-wool refuseniks. The pairing is, at any rate, polemical. That's often why it is disliked. Those in favor are unhappy with half measures, such as a transparent kneesock, but they tremble with delight over "real" socks. You're afraid it will have a Bozo-the-Clown effect? Adapt the color of your socks to the color of your pumps or clothes. Example: Bordeaux pumps + Bordeaux socks + gray pants; red pumps + navy socks + navy dress. You're also allowed to wear satin-stitched, lace, or Lurex socks to complement your shoes.

Karl Lagerfeld voted in the yes column with his Spring/Summer 2014 collection, which featured pumps worn with socks. Hitting two birds with one stone, he boosted the profile of both these accessories.

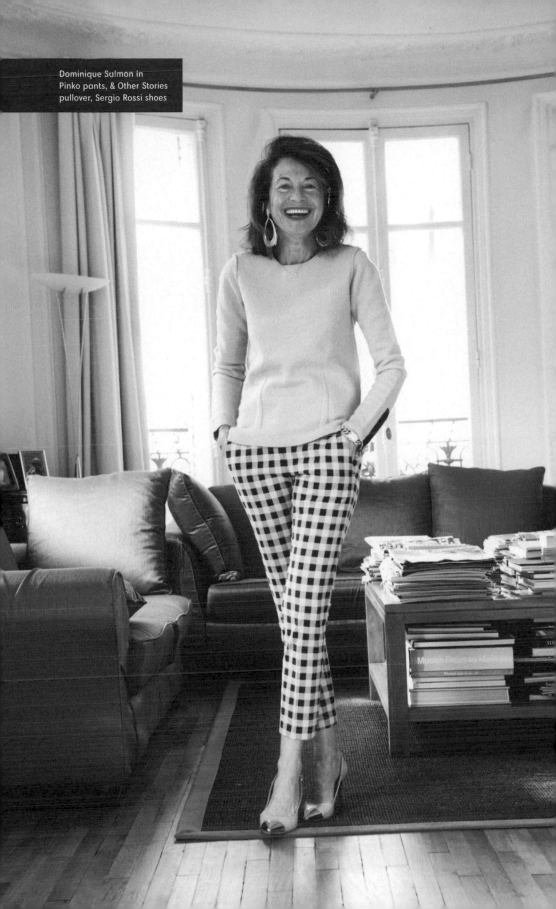

Dominique Salmon in
Pinko pants, & Other Stories
pullover, Sergio Rossi shoes

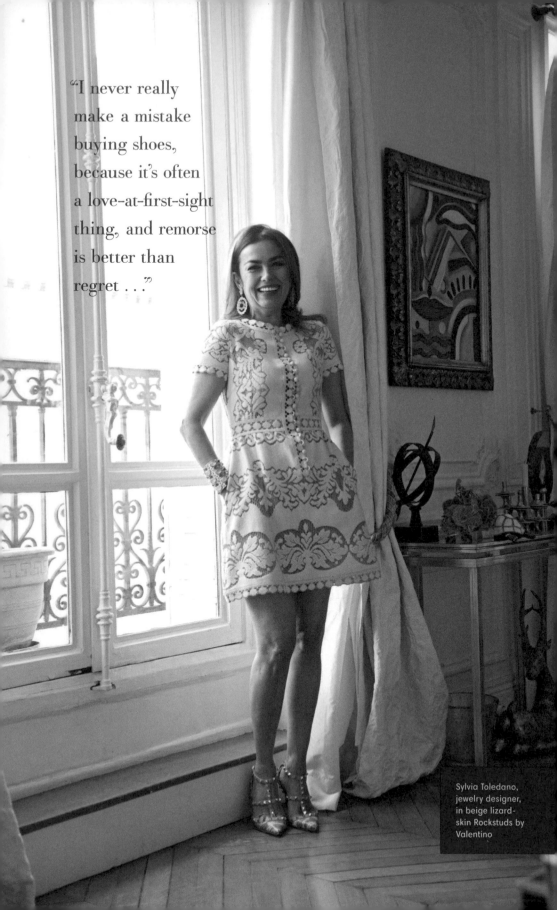

"I never really make a mistake buying shoes, because it's often a love-at-first-sight thing, and remorse is better than regret . . ."

Sylvia Toledano, jewelry designer, in beige lizard-skin Rockstuds by Valentino

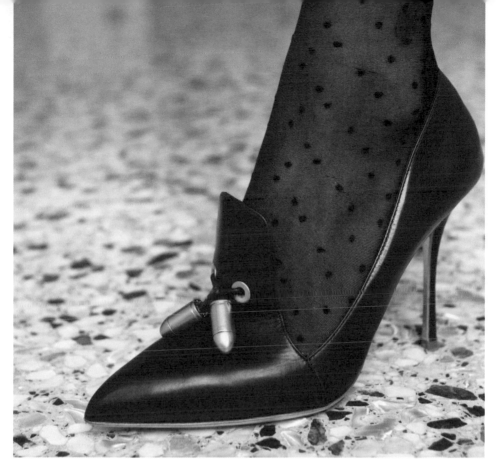

Pumps by Rupert Sanderson

HOW DO YOU GO ALL DAY IN PUMPS?

The problem—if there is one—is an individual matter. While sturdier feet can last all day in heels and pointy toes, others are more sensitive to chafing and want to be released several times a day. That's not always possible. When you're required to wear elegant shoes to work, it's best not to skimp on quality. Obviously. And don't forget to pick a heel height that you are comfortable with. However, comfort isn't always a function of height: Also pay attention to the curve of the sole at the shoe's waist (between the heel and ball of the foot) and the shoe's width, as well as the suppleness of the leather. If resting your feet during the day is an option, slip a pair of ballerinas into your handbag: The Bagllerina was made exactly for this.

A Tip about Chafing

Coat the sensitive area with a little anti-blister cream (e.g., Dr. Scholl's) or stick a Band-Aid inside the shoe over the problem spot.

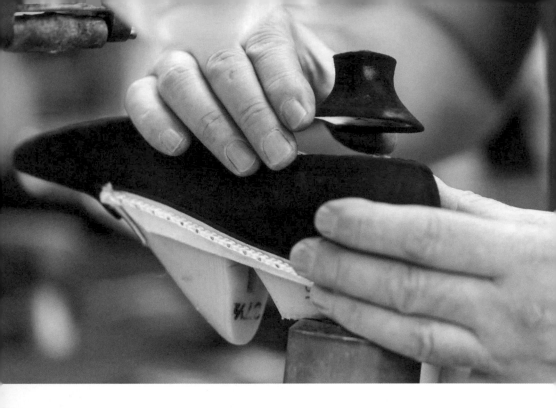

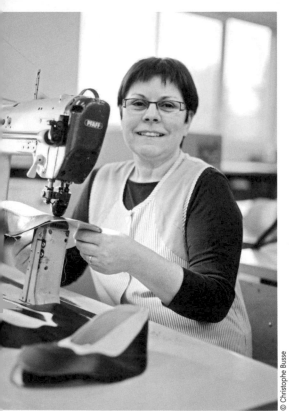

© Christophe Busse

DELAGE

This very prestigious French company, founded in 1991 by the color-savvy duo of Barbara Wirth and Primrose Bordier, is constantly being begged to "keep it small" by its clients, who want to keep the brand all to themselves.

Given three or four weeks' notice, Delage can fabricate your dream shoes for you no matter if it's in iguana, ostrich, sharkskin, python, or crocodile… "One of our most faithful clients, who lives in the Bahamas, regularly orders her favorite shoe in more than 50 different leathers and colors," says Véronique Leremboure, who runs the store in the Palais-Royal in Paris.

This French-made line of shoes—it is actually manufactured in Brittany—is aimed at a clientele that values confidentiality and is unimpressed by recognizable logos.

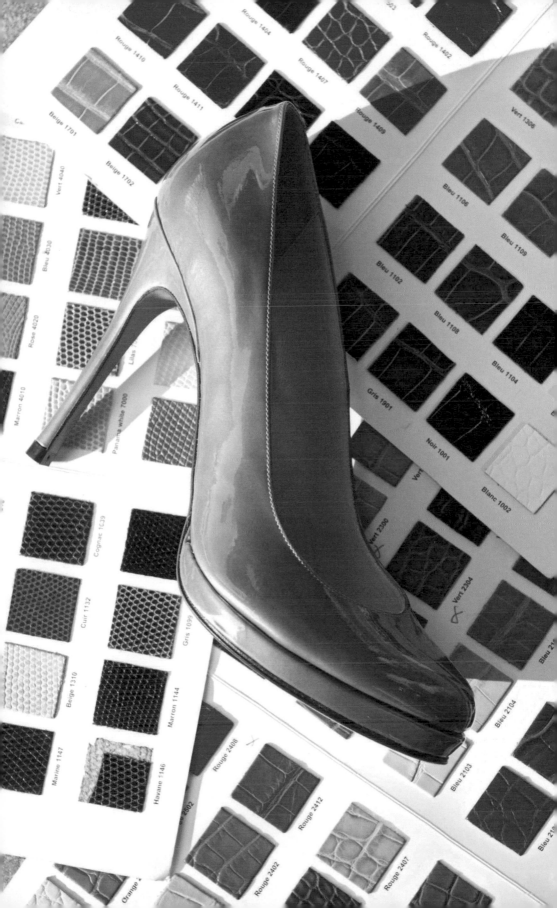

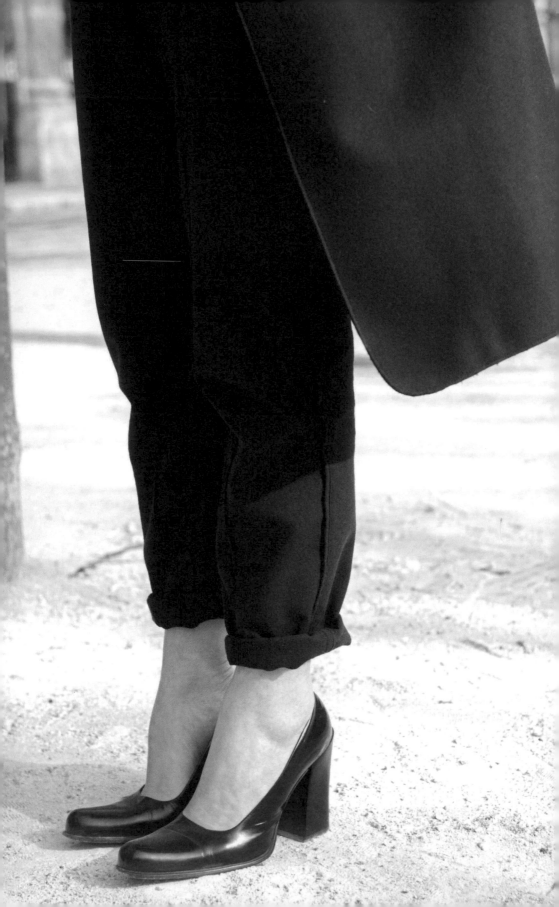

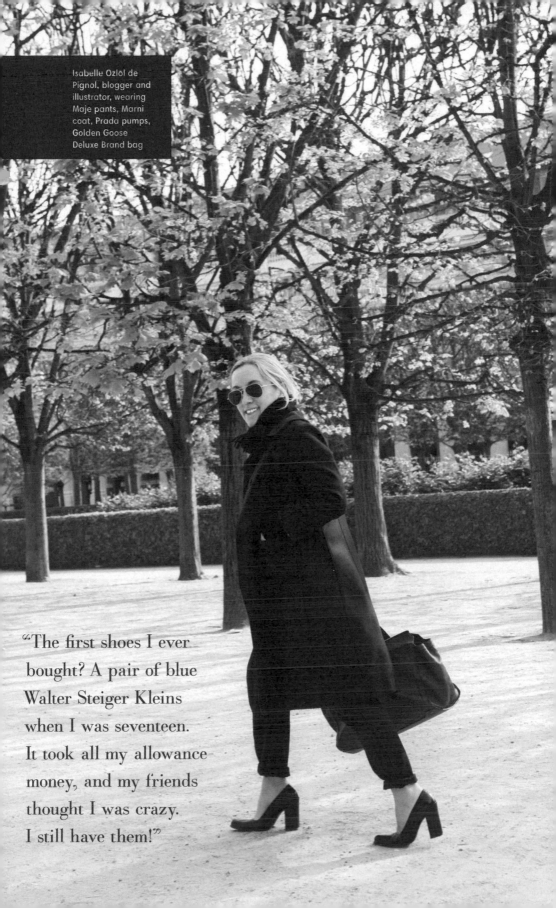

"The first shoes I ever bought? A pair of blue Walter Steiger Kleins when I was seventeen. It took all my allowance money, and my friends thought I was crazy. I still have them!"

My Favorite Shoes

· · · · · · · · · · · · · · · · · ·

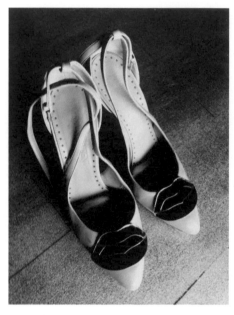

EMMANUELLE SEIGNIER

"These shoes were given to me by Tom Ford when he was at Yves Saint Laurent. They have a link with Roman [Polanski] and the success of *The Pianist*. I wore them, for instance, to the Césars award ceremony."

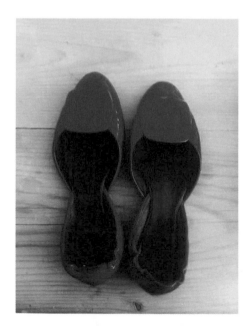

MARIANNE FAITHFULL

"They are elegant, I wear them on stage and to honor *The Red Shoes* by director Michael Powell."

JULIETTE SWILDENS

"What I like best is to have things that are one of a kind! Oxfords never go out of fashion: They're chic, they're masculine and feminine, they're the shoes that are most like me.

These are a style from a Swildens collection, made of snakeskin, and only one pair was made. I like the idea that I'm the only person to have them!

That's why I often have vintage things... Otherwise, I'm lucky that I can wear the prototypes of shoes before they're manufactured!"

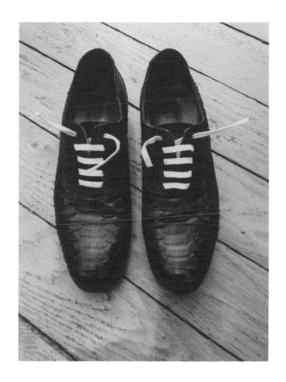

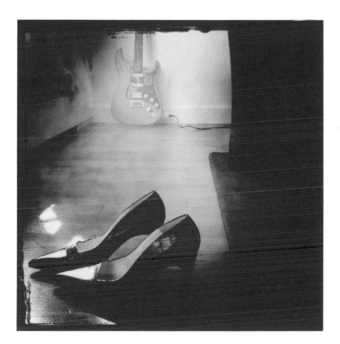

HELENA NOGUERRA

"My Dries Van Noten pumps. They were given to me by the man I love. They make me feel like Cinderella. I've finally found a shoe to fit my foot."

My Favorite Shoes

· · · · · · · · · · · · · · · ·

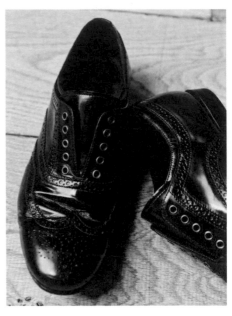

VIRGINIE LEDOYEN

"A present from Prada, ages ago, I adore them. They go with everything and make me feel good."

JOSÉPHINE DRAÏ'S SPARKLY OXFORDS

"And here are the shoes I just can't get rid of! They come from New York, a modest store.... They remind me so much of Michael Jackson during the Billie Jean period that although they're completely shot (sole coming unglued, edges held together with Super Glue), I feel stylish wearing them!"

INÈS DE LA FRESSANGE

"The more things you own, the more you question yourself about what's essential.

On paper, what you'd like is:

- something sophisticated
- something classic
- something not too dreary
- something that goes with everything
- something you could wear day or night
- something elegant but rock 'n' roll
- something comfortable

And all that, of course, in the same item!

My little Maréchal slippers from Roger Vivier have all these qualities. They seem vintage and make me think of the house slippers of a British lord, but they are unmistakably contemporary. With my uniform (navy blue jacket and white jeans), they look impeccable and make my day dressier.

I know they'll still be pretty when they're old, and that's rare for a woman's shoe!"

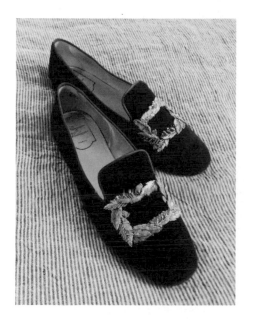

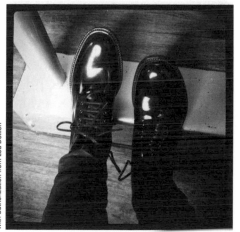

With authorization from Lou Doillon

LOU DOILLON'S SAINT LAURENT BOOTS

Judging from Lou Doillon's Instagram pictures, she feels a boundless devotion to her ankle boots by Hedi Slimane from the first Yves Saint Laurent Paris collection. Or so it would seem from the way she photographs, draws, pampers, and talks to them. Black, lightly varnished, classically androgynous and timeless, these Italian-made boots are already iconic.

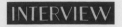

Philippe Atienza

DIRECTOR OF MAISON MASSARO

· · · · · · · · · · · · · · · · ·

"Women are not necessarily faithful to one supplier, but they have several suppliers to whom they are faithful," says Philippe Atienza, head of the famous Maison Massaro, founded in 1894 on the rue de la Paix in Paris. The company, which entered Chanel's fold in 2002, continues to collaborate with the greatest couturiers and to provide elegant women with shoes as lovely as jewels.

How did you become a shoemaker?

A bit by accident, mostly because I liked to ride horseback and wanted a profession related to riding. Riding boots were my point of departure. I started as a journeyman at sixteen, worked in every part of France, slowly climbing the ladder, then worked for more than twenty years at John Lobb. Finally, the Maison Massaro called me to join them in 2008.

How many hours of work does a shoe by Massaro represent?

It depends on the style, but the hands-on work takes thirty to forty hours. By comparison, an industrially made shoe might take twenty to thirty minutes. We have fourteen people working in our ateliers. It takes about two weeks to get an appointment, then we discuss the style of shoe with the client. When we are making a shoe to go with a specific outfit, we develop the design in tandem with the dressmaker. Sometimes, the client brings in a sample of fabric. She might ask our advice, but I don't impose my views. The first step is the design, then we take measurements. Then comes the work on the last, which is entirely carved by hand, then we do a trial model, and the main revisions and corrections are made to this intermediate shoe. Once the model has been revised and approved, we make the final shoe. When it is finished, slight changes can still be made, because a shoe is a little like a racing car: The fit—which can be compared to the motor—has to be adjusted to within a millimeter.

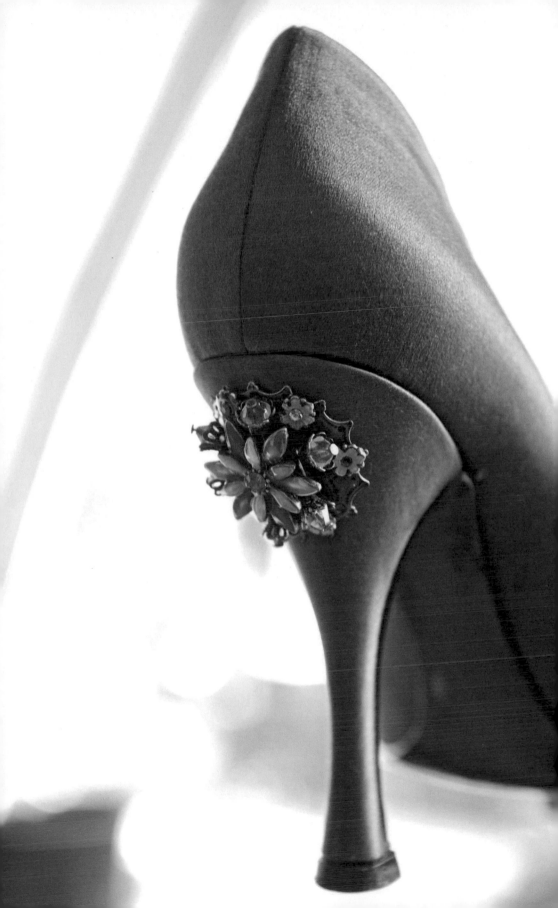

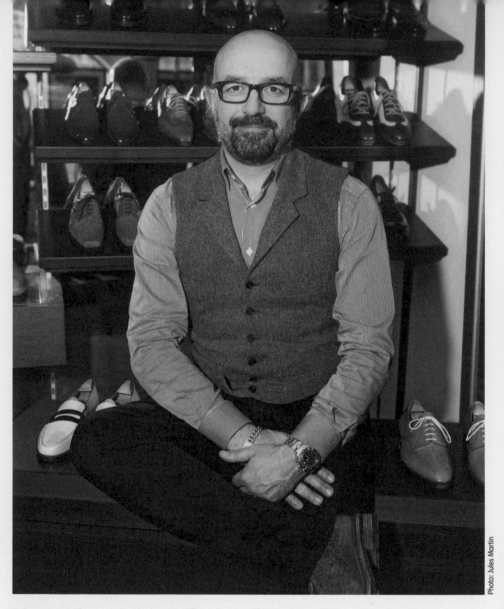

Photo: Jules Martin

"A good number of our clients are women who are tired of filling their closets with shoes they will only wear once. They prefer to pay a high price, knowing they will have fewer shoes but of good quality— shoes they are sure to wear ... and that correspond to their dreams!"

How might a woman recognize a beautiful shoe?

For professionals, many elements come into play, because the quality is revealed at every stage of the process: the last, the footbed, the cutting, and assembly of the upper.

For the consumer, it's more difficult. Naturally, the external aspects of the shoe count—the quality of the leather, the comfort—but it's also a question of educating a person about "the beautiful." Someone with means, a lottery winner, who comes to Massaro to have a pair of shoes made will learn little by little, through comparison, to distinguish between a quality shoe and the other kind.

Have techniques changed in the last thirty years?

The techniques are the same. On the other hand, we are prohibited from using certain products, certain very polluting coloring agents, and I consider it a step forward for the environment. It's our job to adapt to these changes. Take, for example, neoprene glue. It is slated for proscription and will be replaced by a water-based glue that is weaker but also less toxic. It means that the quality will decline, but our environmental impact is important. I don't agree with the attitude that what happened before was always better.

Are there feet that were made for heels?

Not all women can wear very high heels; it depends on the bone structure of their feet. The curve of the foot must be adapted to the curve of the shoe, which is to say, the foot should "marry" this curve, without any gaps; otherwise it will slip toward the front of the shoe, which can cause discomfort and injury. The more arched a foot is, the higher the heel can be—recognizing that it's more complicated to make a very high heel for a small shoe size, say a woman's size five.

I have a client who is over eighty who still wears six-and-a-half-inch heels! [*Philippe Atienza displayed a pair of black thigh-high boots with enormously high heels, destined for this fortunate client.*]

The ideal pair of heels is one that is comfortable at the same time as having a lovely shape. For that to happen, the foot has to find its "space." The front part of the shoe must not be too short, so that all the joints and the big toe can rest on the ground as they should without being curled up or compressed. The wearer must be stable on the ground, standing in a uniform and coherent fashion. The higher the curve, the shorter the shoe's front and the lower the cut.

Do men and women have a different approach toward shoes?

Women are interested above all in style, in appearance. When they get new shoes the first thing they do is to look at themselves in the mirror. Then they are interested in comfort. Many women buy shoes that don't necessarily fit them but which they have fallen for.

A good number of our clients are women who are tired of filling their closets with shoes they will only wear once. They prefer to pay a high price, knowing they will have fewer shoes but of good quality—shoes they are sure to wear… and that correspond to their dreams!

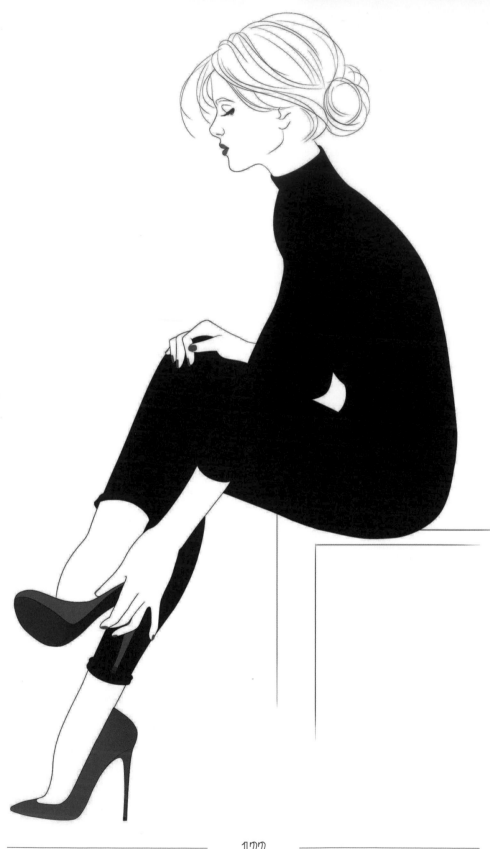

SHOP
LIKE A FRENCH WOMAN

. . . .

Looked at globally, women are not all equal before the great goddess of high heels. Some are constantly making offerings and sacrifices, while others are only moderate in their devotion. French women, who are spoiled when it comes to fashion, buy on average eight pairs a year, which makes us the second largest market for shoes in the world, after the United States.

Established brands, young designers, and everything in between can be found in Paris, making it a tempting and essential fashion center. With 34,500 square feet of retail space dedicated to shoes, the Galeries Lafayette in the heart of Paris offers shoe lovers the largest space in Europe!

Janine Botelho, who runs the shoe department at Printemps on Haussmann Boulevard, another Parisian temple to shoes, tells us that the store sells a pair of women's shoes every five seconds during the first days of a sale.

"You hear them charging up the stairs at a run! They might have to stand in line outside for two or three hours, in blowing wind or driving snow, just to get half off," she says.

The idea of a bargain makes some customers lose their heads to the point where they buy shoes that are too small for them and will therefore never wear, or they come to blows with another shopper who has picked the shoe they wanted for themselves!

But according to Botelho, who sees shoe buyers from all over the world at Printemps, the French woman is the most reasonable and puts comfort and quality ahead of everything else. "French women are afraid of being vulgar," says Botelho. "They buy classic models, because they're unwilling to go out on a limb, and they stick to shoes whose value is well known: simple things, basic things, and in neutral colors like camel, which goes with everything. Recently, French customers have grown more picky about how a shoe is made. They are willing to pay a high price, but the quality must be there."

This change in buying habits is no doubt due to the financial crisis, but also to the realization that the price of clothing and accessories does not always reflect the manufacturing costs. The recent scandals about working conditions in the textile industry have awakened distrust and suspicion in shoe buyers. Being fashionable is one thing, being tricked is another! "Paying big money for a product made in Morocco

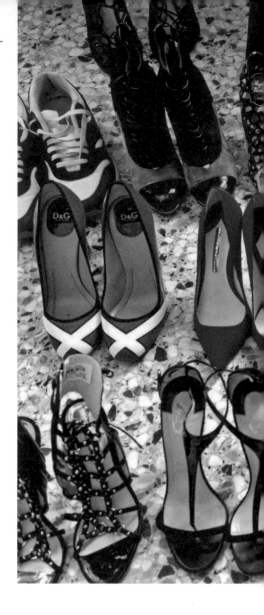

or Tunisia, that's outrageous," says the young designer Fred Marzo, who takes pride in offering beautiful shoes manufactured in France.

Not to say that in summer French women can't be tempted by a colorful or an entirely new design, but they return in winter to more staid and easily paired models. "This is due to France's long winter, which lasts almost eight months. So a pair of winter boots or shoes has to last and be wearable for that whole time," explains Botelho.

And what about men? What do the men who accompany women customers think? "They have very little patience, love heels, and hate UGGs or any heavy or unsightly shoes. 'You're not going to buy that, are you?' is often heard. But Parisian women buy what they like, do as they please, and ignore their husband!," says Botelho.

The international fad of the moment that seems to have everyone on the same wavelength? Nude shoes. "We are selling more and more of them, but beware of going too far toward pink, it has a little girl quality, or toward beige, which has a granny look," Botelho warns.

"I think you could say I'm a collector—a collector who wears her collection into town on a daily basis. Shoes are alive."

CLAIRE MARIE ROCHETTE, BANK MANAGER

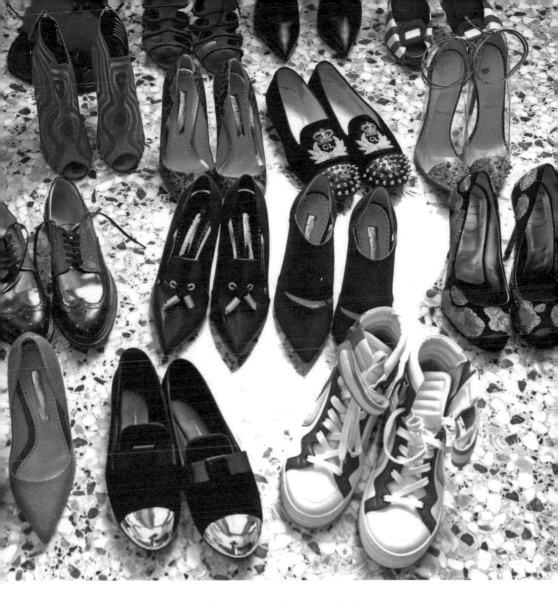

Anne-Sophie Mignaux's extraordinary shoe collection

"French women are afraid of being vulgar. They buy classic models, because they're unwilling to go out on a limb, and they stick to shoes whose value is well known: simple things, basic things, and in neutral colors like camel, which goes with everything.

JANINE BOTELLO, PRINTEMPS SHOE DEPARTMENT

My Life with Shoes

by **Tonie Behar**

Tonie Behar is a writer, editor, and blogger
(www.comedieromantique.com).

I came across the first shoes that made me dream in childhood, when my mother would go out for the evening and my sister and I would rummage in her closet. Among the shoes from Céline and Charles Jourdan was a fascinating pair of almond and green python-skin sandals made by Roger Vivier. Arched above a very high heel of varnished black wood, they seemed to belong to a mysterious world of summer parties, flowing dresses, and golden legs. Through their refined arch, powdery color, and animal matter, they spoke to us of femininity, seduction, and glamour.

Later, when I started working, I fell in love with pretty shoes all over again. Of course, when a girl's growth stops at five foot two, high heels quickly become a precious ally. Especially if you work in fashion and are constantly meeting models who peer down at you from the clouds! I was a press attaché at Emanuel Ungaro, and my boss, who was no taller than I, collected Manolo Blahniks. I didn't like her much, but I

loved her shoes! I became, in turn, one of those chicks who can run all over Paris jacked up on four-inch heels. Even today, whether it's stairs, restaurants, parties, offices, or subway corridors—nothing stops me!

I wore through a good number, threw as many away, and I kept the best ones, the ones that pop out, that rise above the ordinary, like these yellow and brown T-straps from Christian Dior (see page 129), and these evening sandals by Sonia Rykiel in cocoa satin with a marabou pom-pom (see page 128). But, above all, I have a passion for high-heeled boots, in leather or suede, and of every color possible, which I like to wear with everything (dresses, slim jeans), as long as they lift me up and give me style! I like shoes so much that I talk about them in all my novels. My last heroine, Doria, is a girl in a hurry, broke, very rock 'n' roll, and blowing all the money she doesn't have on high-heeled boots…

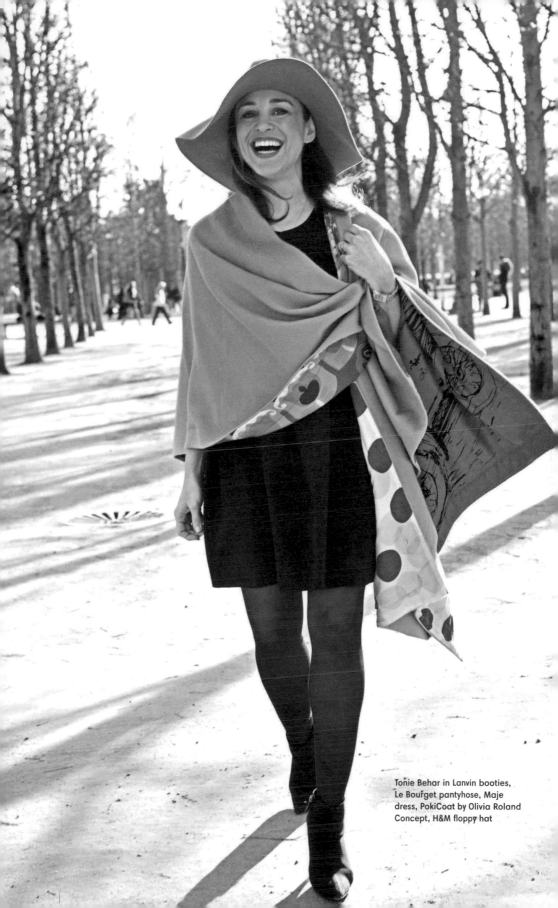

Tonie Behar in Lanvin booties,
Le Bourget pantyhose, Maje
dress, PokiCoat by Olivia Roland
Concept, H&M floppy hat

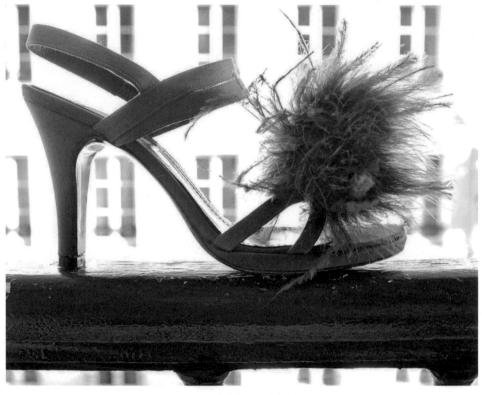

Sonia Rykiel sandal

Opposite: Christian Dior pump

When my second novel came out, the aptly titled *Coups bas et talons hauts* (Low blows and high heels), my publishers sent me around France to take part in several book fairs, and I considered how to get myself noticed among the rows and rows of authors waiting to sign their books. A girlfriend had lent me a pair of spectacular stiletto heels—they were about five inches high, Pradas, made of pale pink satin trimmed with black lace. I set them in plain view on a pile of my books, and it worked: Women would stop to look at the shoes and leave carrying my novel!

Today I own around one hundred pairs of shoes, counting the flip-flops and rubber boots! I know that I'm a small player compared to some other shoe maniacs, with their custom shelves and three hundred or four hundred pairs at the very least, but on days when I'm blue, as I'm organizing my closet and I look at all my little shoes neatly lined up, I almost feel I've made a success of my life!

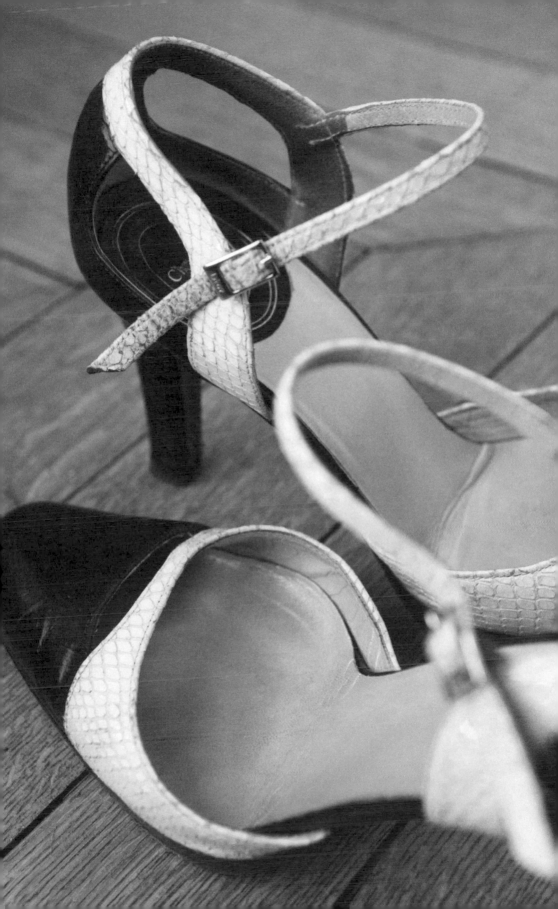

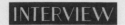

François Najar

FOUNDER OF THE BRAND FRANÇOIS NAJAR

Having seen too many women grimacing from the pain of an aggressive pair of stilettos, François Najar decided to create a high-heeled shoe that would be chic, sexy, and ... comfortable. His credo is the Louis XV heel.

So it's possible to combine stylish design, height, and comfort?

I wanted to go against the current that was giving pride of place to aesthetics. I find that women are more beautiful in heels ... on the condition of not being in pain. I've designed pumps that respect the shape of the foot and don't give you the feeling of walking on three-and-a-half-inch heels but on two-inch heels. A more generous fit and a very particular curve allow you not to worry about sore spots, blisters, or scrunched toes.

Why have you chosen to focus exclusively on the Louis XV heel?

I was looking for a pure and timeless pump that would enhance the wardrobe of a confident, independent woman in search of elegance, a woman as much at ease in a suit as in jeans. It could be [the journalist] Claire Chazal, Sophie Marceau, Charlotte Gainsbourg, you, my mother ... For me, the Louis XV heel is the quintessence of these aspects of urban chic. It's the purest and most elegant heel. But also the most complicated to make. It takes traditional artisanal know-how. For that reason, my shoes are manufactured in Veneto, Italy, the birthplace of the luxury shoe, in an atelier that makes only Louis XV heels.

What would you say to a woman who is afraid of trying heels?

There is nothing in life you can't learn! All it takes is a little practice. Don't start with heels that are too low, go right to two-and-three-quarter-inch heels. Walk around at home, back and forth, go up and down the stairs. And remind yourself that heels change your silhouette, your profile, the arch of your back, the shape of your leg, and your attitude. Wearing heels, you feel more womanly, more desired ... Isn't it a pleasure to answer to these feminine codes?

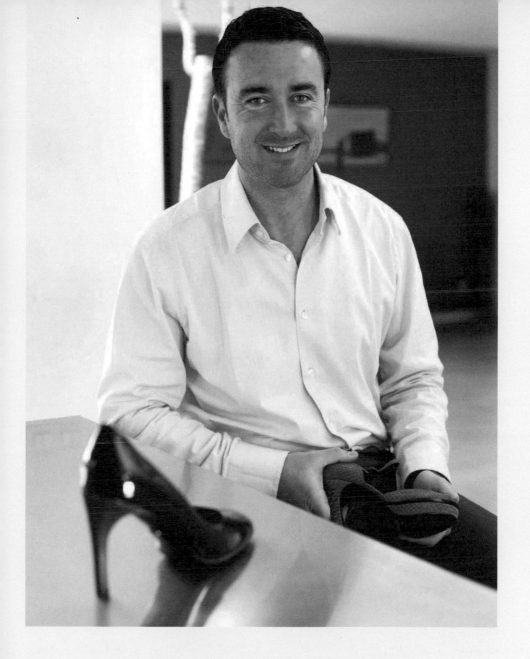

What is the Louis XV heel?

Created by shoemakers in the sixteenth century, it features a heel with a concave profile that gently marries the outer sole.

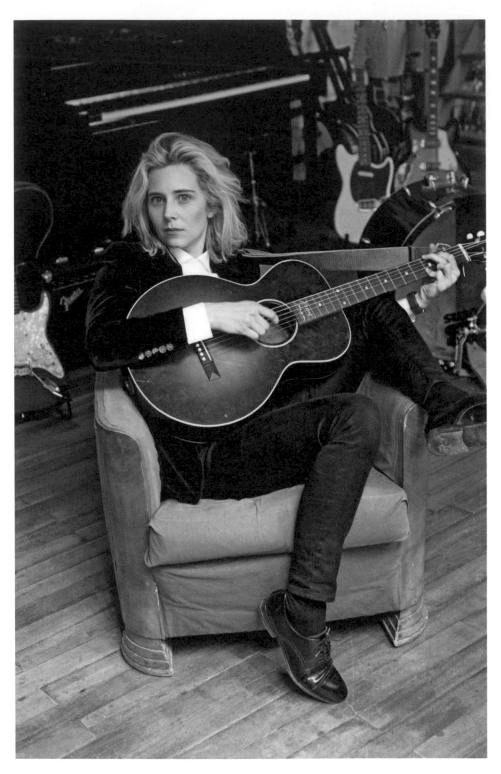

Clémence Gabriel—singer for the band Paul, Théodore, & Gabriel—in Paul Smith shoes

MASCULINE
CAN BE FEMININE

· · · · · · · · · · · · · · · ·

You can be crazy about skyscraper heels but not want to spend your whole life perched on high. Many women have told us this: "I have spectacular heels that I never wear; I just don't have the lifestyle that goes with them." If you live a hectic life, you need to be able to run after the bus and take big strides without feeling as though you're teetering on stilts. You can still buy heels just for the pleasure of looking at them or because you want to own a beautiful object. But you can also be feminine and elegant in shoes other than heels or ballerinas. There is a wide choice of options, from moccasins to brogues, by way of oxfords.

Moccasins are comfortable and enveloping. They were inspired by the deerskin moccasin of the American Indian and were first copied by early immigrants. Then they became a classic item for men as well as women. We like the classic Weston, which wears extraordinarily well; the famous penny loafer; and the mythic Weejun by Bass, worn by James Dean, Michael Jackson… and us!

It was around the 1920s that women's feet were freed and allowed to be shod in something other than laced booties or delicate pumps. Finally they would have the right to a little comfort! In old Europe, only working-class women wore practical shoes. But now, elegant women can venture beyond the drawing room, the boudoir, and the ballroom to discover the

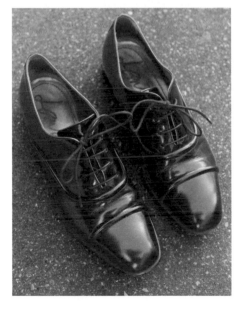

Lanvin shoes

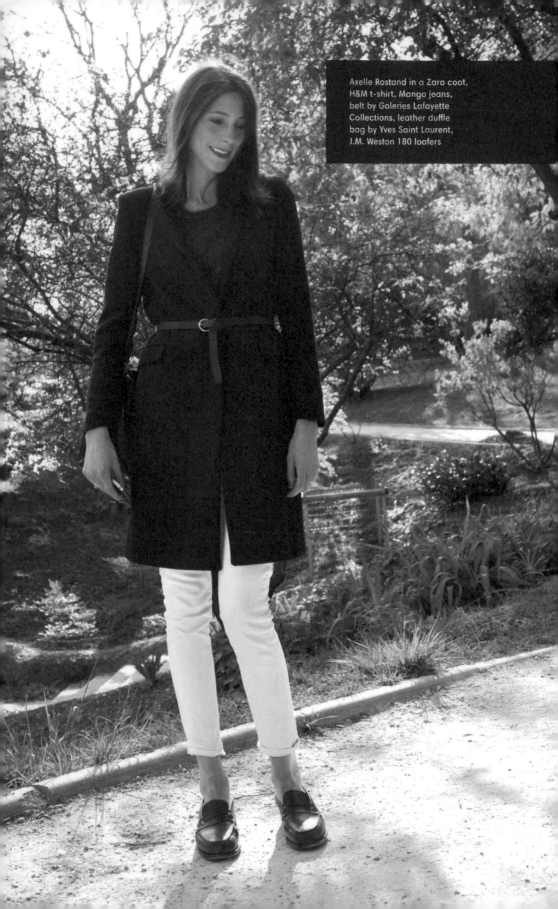

Axelle Rostand in a Zara coat,
H&M t-shirt, Mango jeans,
belt by Galeries Lafayette
Collections, leather duffle
bag by Yves Saint Laurent,
J.M. Weston 180 loafers

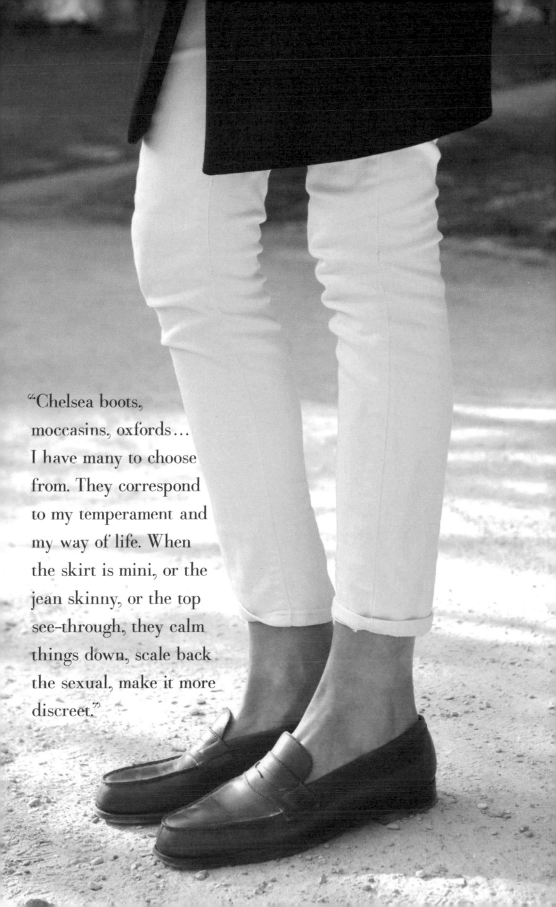

"Chelsea boots, moccasins, oxfords… I have many to choose from. They correspond to my temperament and my way of life. When the skirt is mini, or the jean skinny, or the top see-through, they calm things down, scale back the sexual, make it more discreet."

world in flats. Marlene Dietrich, for instance, was at her most feminine and seductive when she wore men's tails from Savile Row, brogues, and an arrogant cigarette wedged in the corner of her mouth!

Easy-to-wear shoes from a man's closet can go with just about anything. But they don't necessarily suit everyone.

The goal is not to copy the look achieved (oh so well!) by Justin Timberlake, but to move in the direction of Tilda Swinton, who has a genius for gender bending.

The upside: They can introduce some ambiguity into a very feminine outfit.

The downside: Worn with the wrong outfit, men's shoes can make you look like Miss Marple tromping across the Scottish heath.

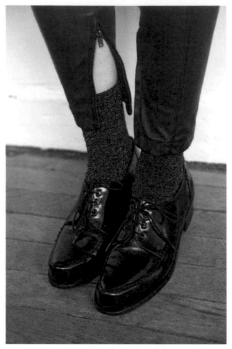

Rock 'n' roll–style boyfriend shoes

"I don't like wearing heels. I've had a couple of times now where I feel like, by the end of the night, when I'm wearing heels at events, my feet feel like they're sitting in pools of blood. And it's really awful."
MARY-KATE OLSEN, *ASOS* MAGAZINE, 2012

· ·

1980

Clergerie opened its doors and successfully launched an oxford that played indisputably on androgyny. With its Goodyear tread, high-quality leather, and careful style, it had all the ingredients to win the hearts of women.

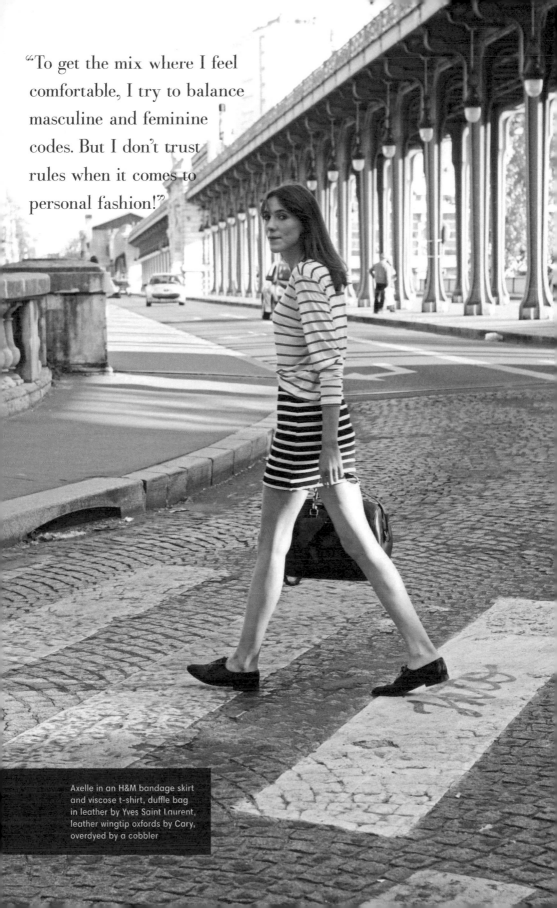

"To get the mix where I feel comfortable, I try to balance masculine and feminine codes. But I don't trust rules when it comes to personal fashion!"

Axelle in an H&M bandage skirt and viscose t-shirt, duffle bag in leather by Yves Saint Laurent, leather wingtip oxfords by Cary, overdyed by a cobbler

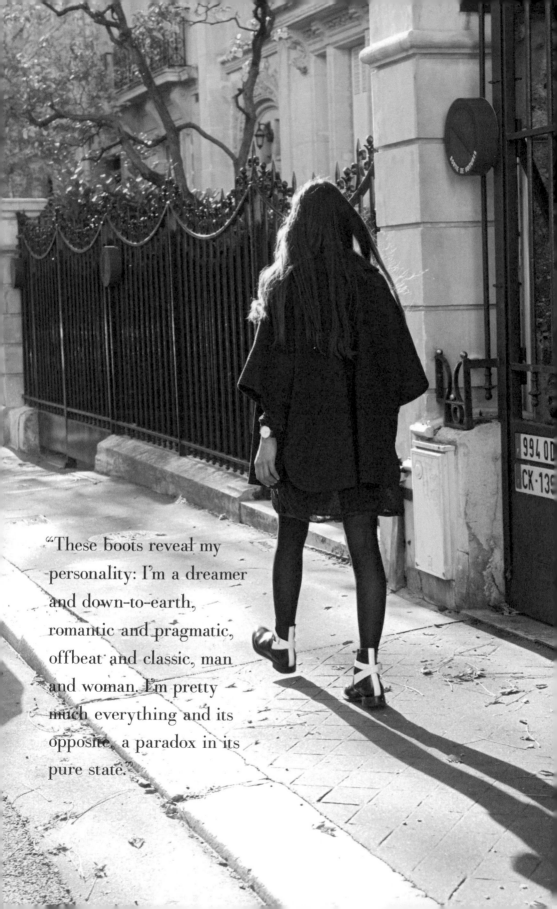

"These boots reveal my personality: I'm a dreamer and down-to-earth, romantic and pragmatic, offbeat and classic, man and woman. I'm pretty much everything and its opposite, a paradox in its pure state."

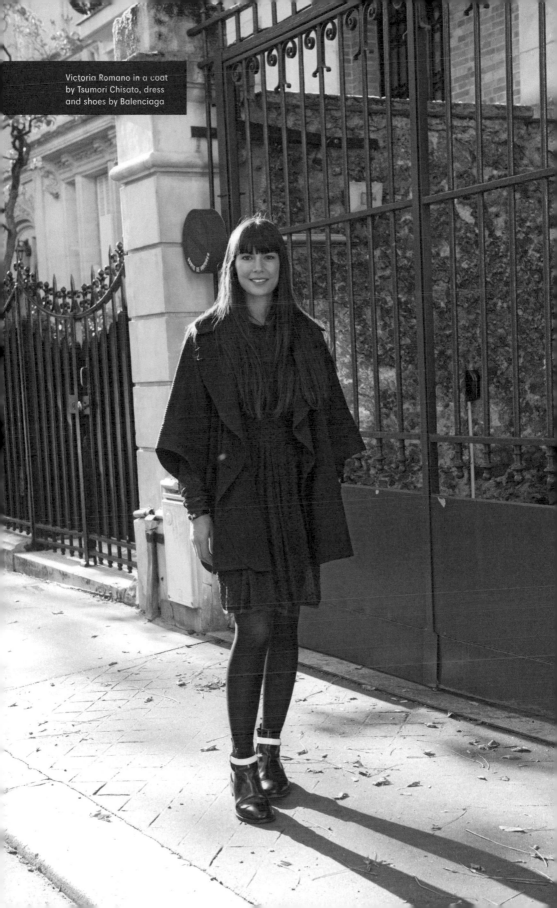

Victoria Romano in a coat by Tsumori Chisato, dress and shoes by Balenciaga

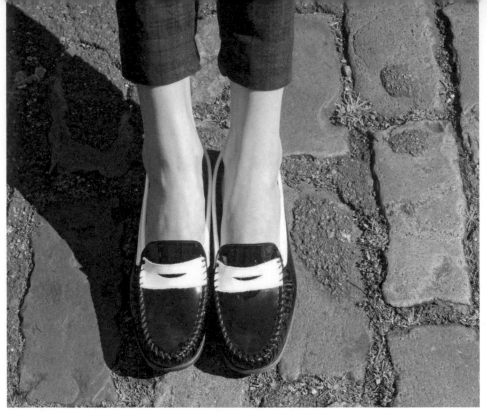

Two-toned loafer by Maurice Manufacture

LUXURY SHOES
MADE IN FRANCE

According to Philippe Granger of Maurice Manufacture, a company that produces all of its shoes entirely in France, finding shoes made in France is rare but worth the extra effort and cost.

"In the old days, women's luxury shoes in France were represented by Clergerie, Kélian, and Jourdan. These companies designed and made their own shoes. Today most of the shoe manufacturers have left France. In the late 1980s, there was a gap in time between the deaths of Kélian, of Jourdan, and the moment when luxury brands started offering shoes as accessories. All the luxury fashion houses like Chanel, Dior...began by offering products from Italian companies, because they had the know-how, but also because the shoe industry was dying in France. The shoes offered by these luxury brands were immediately popular, which nobody had predicted.

"When Vuitton entered the shoe business, it applied the economic model it had used for its luggage business and quickly abandoned the plan of having its shoes made in France. There wasn't a single company able to leap into production in response to the large demand of the luxury market. Jourdan and Kélian didn't have the corporate culture to manufacture for outside companies. Today the bulk of the luxury shoe market is in the hands of companies that didn't originally make shoes."

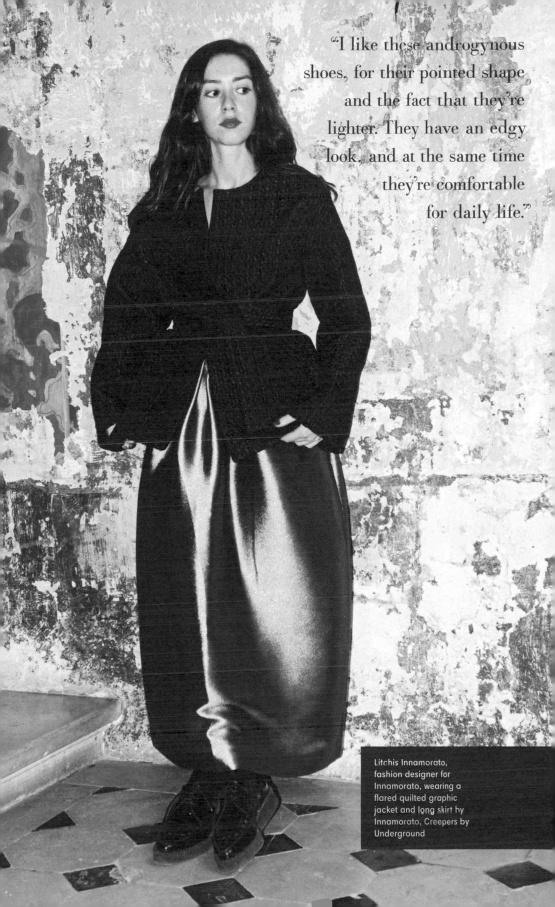

"I like these androgynous shoes, for their pointed shape and the fact that they're lighter. They have an edgy look, and at the same time they're comfortable for daily life."

Litchis Innamorato, fashion designer for Innamorato, wearing a flared quilted graphic jacket and long skirt hy Innamorato, Creepers by Underground

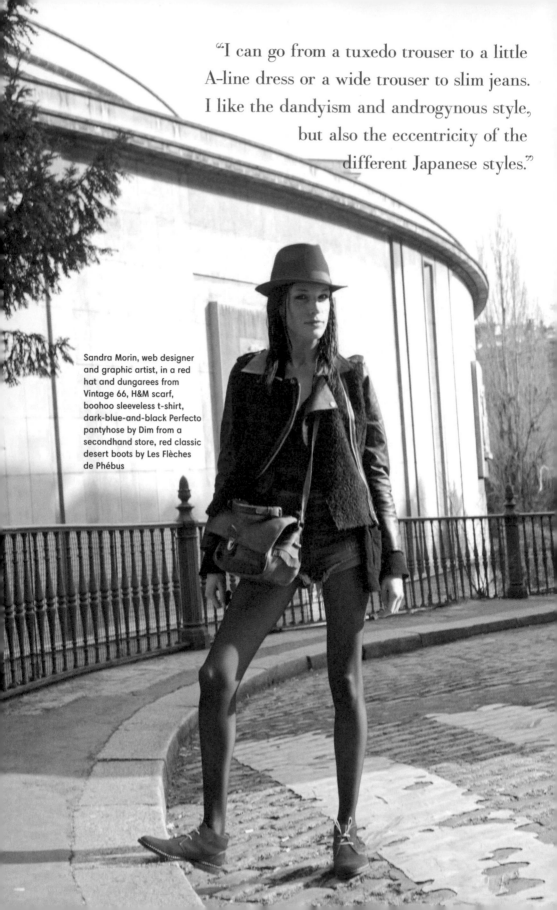

"I can go from a tuxedo trouser to a little A-line dress or a wide trouser to slim jeans. I like the dandyism and androgynous style, but also the eccentricity of the different Japanese styles."

Sandra Morin, web designer and graphic artist, in a red hat and dungarees from Vintage 66, H&M scarf, boohoo sleeveless t-shirt, dark-blue-and-black Perfecto pantyhose by Dim from a secondhand store, red classic desert boots by Les Flèches de Phébus

THE EIGHT COMMANDMENTS OF WEARING GUYS' SHOES

1. If you are drawn to masculine styles, we encourage you to choose shoes with a slightly fantastic element: oxfords with two colors, studs, a leopard pattern, or python skin...

2. If you are short or have round calves, avoid very thin soles; they will make you seem shorter. A hint: When wearing trousers with a narrow leg, roll up the cuff to reveal your ankle and elongate your figure. Or wear cropped pants.

3. Wear men's shoes in their original version with a dressy suit but complemented by a t-shirt with graphics or a blue denim shirt. Or, again, wear them with wide, high-waisted pants + a low-cut white shirt. The secret is to play up the feminine/masculine opposition by inserting a feminine touch—some lace or see-through fabric—to make the outfit mysterious and provocative.

4. Offset the shoes with an over-the-knee sheath dress, a leather pencil skirt + silk shirt, a flowing dress that falls to the ankles, or kidskin shorts + blazer.

5. The preppy look is not for you? Forget about wearing your bluchers with college-student clothes à la Alexa Chung (shorts or short skirt + ankle socks) and raise the ante with a skirt that comes below the knee + a vest belted at the waist, or a high-waisted pencil skirt + a short mohair pullover. Or choose the glam rock version: slim leather pants + loose t-shirt + tuxedo jacket.

6. So as not to contribute to a caricature of middle-class complacency, moccasins should be of the penny-loafer variety (not to be confused with boat shoes!). Wear your moccasins with a pant that narrows at the ankle, a sailor's shirt, and a blazer. Add colored socks to give the whole look a little wit and femininity.

7. Are you worried that your men's shoes will look too serious, and combining them with jeans seems boring? Wear them with printed or brocaded pants, or with a pantsuit that has vivid stripes or a flower pattern.

8. Guys' shoes don't get along with lightweight pantyhose, but they hit it off well with brightly colored Lurex or printed ankle socks and with woolen tights. And they're OK with bare feet.

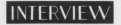

Robert Clergerie

SHOEMAKER

• • • • • • • • • • • • • • • • •

He describes himself as the last dinosaur of the profession and likes to repeat a maxim of André Perugia's on man's vital dependence on his shoes, concluding that a shoe must be comfortable and, of course, elegant. This young man, born in 1934, has never lost his love for beautiful shoes.

How did you start in the shoe business?

It's a long story! My father was a grocer in Levallois-Perret. I spent my childhood there. As I was a good student, I passed my college exams and studied business administration. I dreamt of adventure, so I decided to go abroad: I took the metro to Louise Michel [station], then the train, then the boat to New York. At the time it was unusual to travel abroad. The crossing took two weeks. We were several in the cabin and, fatefully enough, my bunkmate was a Mexican who sold shoes in France.

From New York, I traveled to Mexico by bus. I was twenty-three years old. I stayed there for several years, living like Gérard Philipe in *The Proud and the Beautiful*, and I had to return to France because the army called me up during the war in Algeria.

When I got back, somewhat low in morale, I answered a want ad from Charles Jourdan and I fell in love with shoes—their volume, shape, material, and the extraordinary leather that goes into them.

You started Clergerie in the 1980s?

The Clergerie brand was created in 1981, but I had bought a men's shoe company long before: UNIC, started in the nineteenth century by Joseph Fenestrier. It was a factory for luxury shoes that used the Goodyear welt process. I sold everything in order to buy this company, and without my wife's support I would never have been able to do anything!

Fenestrier and Charles Jourdan were the two great figures in the shoemaking world. [Stephane] Kélian and I simply followed in their footsteps!

> *"That was the end of the skyscraper heel for several years. Every woman wanted a pair. I even had Lauren Bacall as a client!"*

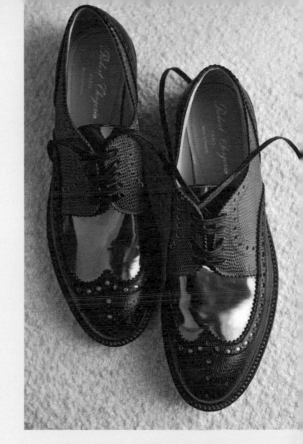

A timeless model from the Clergerie collection

How did you get the idea of making a man's oxford shoe for women?

It was the result of seeing Yves Saint Laurent's runway shows. His models in tuxedos and modified men's suits needed a more masculine shoe, and that's where I got the idea of making a man's shoe for women. A friend, Annie Destin, pointed out to me that I had the factory, the idea, and the name! She encouraged me to start the business. At the time, no one was making mannish shoes for women; it wasn't the fashion. The industry leader was Charles Jourdan with his high heels and the wonderful and provocative ad campaigns by Guy Bourdin.

When I got into the business, heels were no higher than two or two-and-a-half inches; then they got higher. Charles Jourdan even made heels four inches high. At the time, that was a lot! In New York, in the dead of winter with snow on the ground, I saw women entering the Waldorf Astoria in high-heeled sandals!

I launched my first collection with three styles of shoe: Paco, Paris, and Palma—an oxford, a brogue, and a tuxedo pump. I had patent leather, black, white, and two-toned. I was lucky that my first four clients (one of which was Barneys) were world leaders in opinion, and I had immediate success. The press was clamoring for my shoes, so I opened my shop on the rue du Cherche-Midi in Paris. That was the end of the skyscraper heel for several years. Every woman wanted a pair. I even had Lauren Bacall as a client!

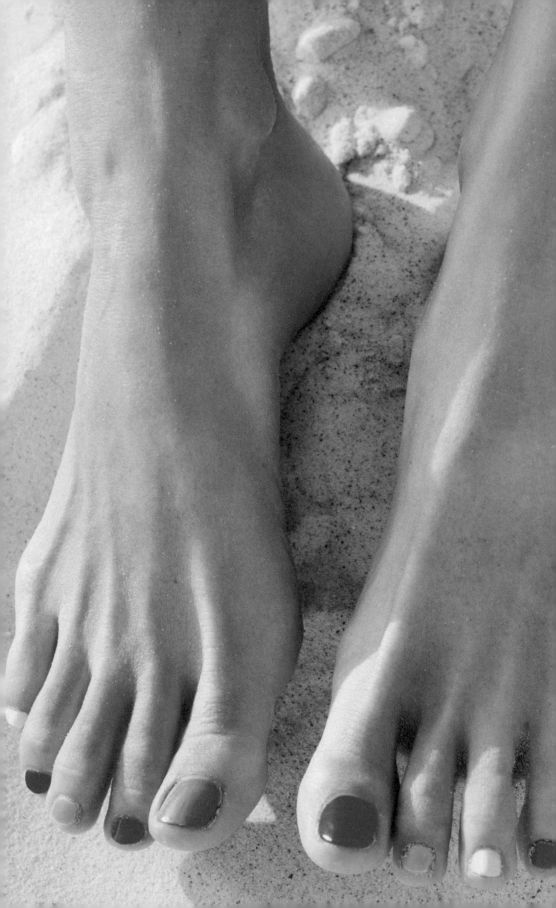

TAKE CARE
OF YOUR FEET!

· · · · · · · · · · · · · · · · · ·

Feet have a strong erotic charge for certain people, while others see them mostly as a source of complexes. "Sausage-like," "elongated," "too pale," "lumpy," "twisted"—they'd rather let them hibernate than reveal them in sandals. Even if no one makes you display your feet, it is very important to take care of them…and you might even become reconciled to them along the way.

We have no problem looking after our hands on a regular basis. By contrast, we often don't pay enough attention to our feet.

"Women generally take an interest in them once a year, before a beach vacation," says Joëlle Levy, a podiatrist and pedicurist. "And yet a regular pedicure—once every three months at least—does a great deal to ward off damage to your feet. Not counting that a nice pedicure helps you like them."

When your feet rub against shoes that are too tight or leather that is too stiff in heels that are wrong for you, it can lead to corns, calluses, ingrown toenails, or bunions. "The problem is that most people choose shoes for their looks and not to fit the shape of their feet," says Levy.

And then there are women who are crazy about high heels. If you wear stilettos regularly, your weight lands on the forward part of your foot and you risk developing calluses as your skin grows tender and eventually thickens at the point of maximum contact.

Joëlle Levy advises against using silicone foot cushions: "It's a placebo that has every chance of being adapted neither to your feet nor to your shoes. It's better to have an orthopedic insole made to your measure and also to spare your feet whenever possible. You don't need to go full bore every day!"

HOW TO GET RID OF CORNS

Levy doesn't recommend over-the-counter corn removal bandages for dealing with painful corns: "The bandage can slip and the salicylic acid it contains can eat away at the healthy skin around the corn. And stay away from those

· ·

Victoria Beckham is said to massage her feet every night to help them cope with the four- and five-inch heels she wears on a daily basis.

"I don't wear make-up, but on the other hand I do wear toenail polish: reds, eggplant purples… I take care of my feet, and people often compliment me on them."

Adeline Roussel

. . . .

implements they sell, which can really hurt you. A corn can't be eliminated with Band-Aids, or with corn trimmers. Only a professional can provide relief."

VARIETY IS THE SPICE OF LIFE

If you always wear athletic shoes, your foot is not supported and will widen. As to soles that are overly thin—those delicate ballet flats!—they provide no cushioning. Avoid them on days when you will be galloping around; you'll be subjecting your spine to repeated shocks and the risk of back pain. The best thing for when you need to run places: crepe soles.

The secret is to alternate between high and low, running shoes, boots, ankle boots, pumps, sandals…. We applaud diversity!

. . . .

MY TOES ARE KILLING ME

A bunion is a deformity that women are prone to and that develops over the course of your life. If your mother complained of them, watch out; it's hereditary. This bony bump at the base of your big toe comes from ill-fitting shoes: shoes that are too pointed, too high, or have straps or a side cut that aggravates the bone cells. "If you feel pain there, it's a sign that the condition is already in progress," says the podiatrist Joëlle Levy.

RECIPE FOR FEET LIKE A BABY'S

Every morning or evening, rub your feet with moisturizing cream—hand cream will do just fine. Every ten days, gently pumice your heels. Don't do it any more often or you will excite the cells of your plantar skin to form more calluses; it's a vicious circle.

If your bone-white feet are giving you a complex, rub them with a gradual self-tanning lotion. You won't risk turning them orange; they'll just develop a light, healthy tan. You can also use a little sun powder.

Victoria Beckham is said to massage her feet every night to help them cope with the four- and five-inch heels she wears on a daily basis.

. . . .

WHAT IS REFLEXOLOGY?

A holistic healing art on par with acupuncture, plantar reflexology is based on the tenet that the foot is divided into zones that each correspond to an organ of the body.

The pressure exerted by a reflexologist can resolve various problems (sleep disorders, digestive or urinary issues) and cure various ailments (recurrent ear infections, backaches) without resorting to medication.

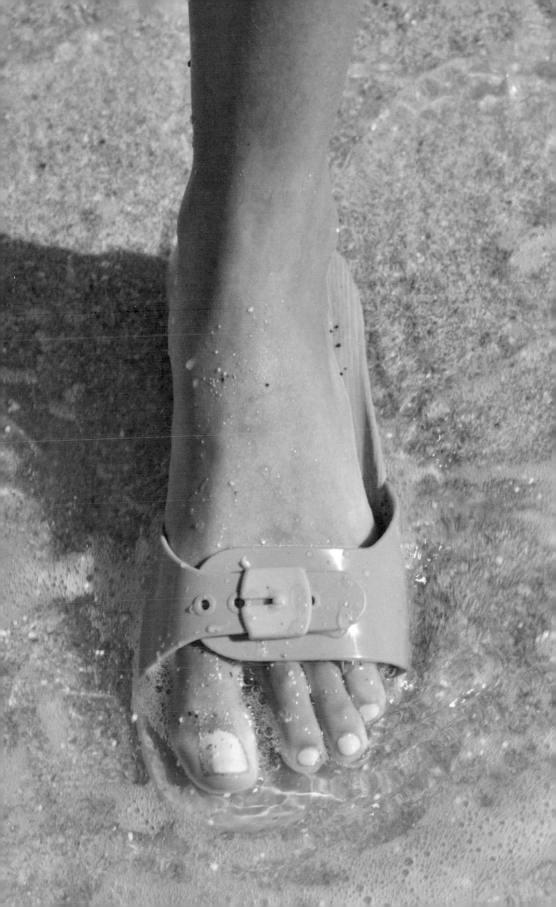

ADVICE FROM LAURENCE C., A REFLEXOLOGIST

"Your feet talk.
Look at them and take care of them."

They are the means we use to get from here to there, the base on which we stand upright. All the more reason not to forget them! When a reflexologist holds our feet in her hands, our feet speak to her about our current problems, our physiological concerns, and incidents from our past. She pays attention to them. As long as there is trust, she and our feet can enter into a dialogue.

What problems do you see from looking at city-dwellers' feet?
Stress brings a systematic set of problems related to sleep, digestion, and urination. I am also noticing more and more issues linked to failed relationships and harassment in the

· ·

"Yes, be kind to your feet. Choose shoes you love, but be considerate to the marvelous instruments that give us mobility."

workplace. I see people who are depressed and unwilling to say so. This applies both to upper-level executives and to a younger generation. And then there are all the complaints due to bad posture: back problems, trick knees... Our feet have always received information from the body and the mind—a plethora of sayings in the language attest to this ("to start off on the right foot," "to trip over one's feet," "to put one's foot in one's mouth," etc.).

If our feet can reveal our problems, can ill-fitting shoes influence our physical and mental state?
The higher your shoes, the more they can injure you. If your weight always falls on one particular area, then yes, you can provoke certain problems. For example, dancers' feet are in deplorable condition: They are always putting pressure on their toes, which, in reflexology, corresponds to the head. There's also the fashion for toe rings. The rings press against certain

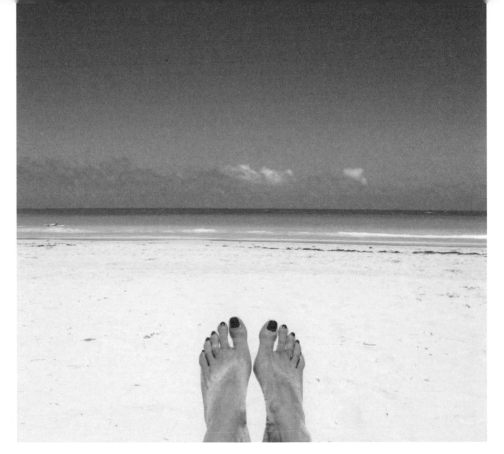

"When my friends ask me for a photograph,
I send them a picture of my feet!"

Adeline Roussel

spots that shouldn't be constantly stimulated. We are not in India, we don't have the same understanding of feet that they have; the practice is not a good one for us.

Can you massage yourself using a reflexology chart?

It's not a good idea. Reading a reflexology chart is not easy for the practitioner, who does it right-side up, so it would be even more of a stretch for you to do upside down. Plus, we don't expect a surgeon to cut open his own stomach. It's better to find the right person and entrust your weary feet to him or her. But it doesn't stop you from keeping an eye on your feet. For example, the location of a corn is not linked only to pressure points but also to the parts of your life that are fragile at any given moment.

Walk barefoot around your own house, paying attention to setting your feet down firmly on the ground… And look at them: Oh, I've got feet! And go without nail polish from time to time; it has a tendency to prevent the nail from breathing. Your toenails represent the surface of your skull. So when you are operated on, they ask you to remove any nail polish. It's not just a question of hygiene; our nails give indications of the reactions inside our bodies.

Yes, be kind to your feet. Choose shoes you love, but be considerate to the marvelous instruments that give us mobility.

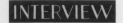

Bruno Frisoni

ARTISTIC DIRECTOR FOR ROGER VIVIER

· · · · · · · · · · · · · · · · · ·

Roger Vivier designed the sandals for the coronation of Elizabeth II, the thigh-highs for Brigitte Bardot on her Harley-Davidson; made shoes for Marlene Dietrich, Wallis Simpson, and Elizabeth Taylor; invented the spike heel, the "shock," and the "comma." With such an impressive history, what's the future for this iconic brand?

For several years, Bruno Frisoni has been rein-terpreting the master's creations with talent and a modern eye. Using exceptional materials, he creates in very small batches. Each client can be certain of owning a shoe or a handbag that exists only in a very limited edition. And that is also of very high quality! Born of Italian parents, Bruno Frisoni has always been atten-tive to the overall look and a certain good taste: "Our sophistication as Italians set us apart. An index of taste, like our cooking!"

Have you always been obsessed with shoes?

In any case, I remember my little one-inch plat-form shoes. I must have been about twelve. I'd had the bad idea of playing on the edge of a river, and my poor shoes unfortunately didn't survive the experience. I never forgot them! But if I had to describe two emblematic styles of women's shoes that made a mark on me, it would be a pair of beige stilettos and a pair of brogues from the 1970s, a little heavy, in bur-gundy leather, with a boot heel of the kind that Hermès makes perfectly. As a child, I thought that I would design jewelry. But between my love of design and of fashion, I found my hap-piness in shoes. In the end, shoe designs are as detailed as for jewelry.

So why this love for shoes?

When you see a person, what you look at are that person's extremities: the hair, the hands, the feet. It's almost more important than the clothes they are wearing. Shoes change your leg, your ankle joint… It's an instrument of seduction. It lets you play with the pleasure of an encounter, the joy of being seduced. And then, shoes are an extension of clothes. You don't wear stilettos with a bathing suit, unless you're still back in the 1980s. A shoe doesn't exist all by itself; it necessarily combines with an outfit.

What woman inspires you when you imagine a shoe?

It changes from season to season. It's a little like playing with dolls. I imagine a hairstyle, a color, a character… My latest imaginary muse is of Greek origin; she lives in London, takes an interest in fashion, and approaches sexy shoes with a cool femininity—as though she were wearing an athletic shoe.

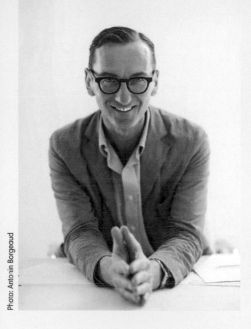

Photo: Antonin Borgeaud

"The perfect shoe does not exist."

of options; you just have to take the time to do your research. Better to be selective than to accumulate poor choices.

It has become easier to make fashion mistakes, no?

The only thing that's in bad taste is to be out of harmony with oneself. Nothing is vulgar or ugly; only situations are. It's the way things are combined that's interesting, not the object itself. You can be bling-bling and still very elegant if you have what it takes. A Charlotte Rampling will never be in bad taste. You have to know whether you can take risks. And then, it's by making mistakes, by doing things in bad taste, that you learn about good taste. All the same, I'd have to eliminate those horrible Crocs: Those gardening shoes with holes are always horrible. I prefer thongs or Swedish clogs, which I love. Even wooden-soled Dr. Scholl's flip-flops with their pretty buckle can be amusing if you have the right leg for it and good shorts.

What does the "French touch" mean to you in terms of fashion?

Today it's almost arrogant and old-fashioned to talk about French elegance. Style is more dynamic than that. Yes, French chic is still admired, but every major city has its own brand of chic. The woman from Milan is more staid, the Tokyoite more conceptual, the Londoner more adventurous… Fashion is a shared culture.

No need to be perched on heels to seduce?

No! Look at Inès de la Fressange. Whether she's wearing men's boots or ultra-feminine shoes, she's attractive, thanks to her tomboy look. She's a player. We all have an interest in understanding the person that we are, in playing good-humoredly with shoes and clothes. We mustn't be the coat hanger for a piece of clothing; we must be ourselves. It's a question of balance. Think of interior decorating: An object can be disastrous in one place and fantastic in another. Shoes are the same way: Something that is too much can be either ridiculous or phenomenal. So there is no such thing as a perfect object.

For the ideal shoe, must you just pay enough money?

It's not because an object, an article of clothing, or a shoe, is inexpensive that it is less good. You can buy an article that costs 2,000 euros and still not be sure that it's going to be better than one that costs 200 euros. Price no longer means anything. Quality, yes. Today, we have the good fortune of having an infinite number

PANTYHOSE AND SOCKS CAN MAKE YOUR LEGS LOOK GREAT

· · · · · · · · · · · · · · · · ·

Choose the wrong ones, and they can ruin your look. You don't wear pantyhose just to keep your legs warm but for some style as well. Follow our lead!

We are absolutely convinced that it is better to break your piggybank to buy a good pair of pantyhose than to get three pairs that are only so-so. Of course, you will sometimes find wonderful things from a small company or a big department store, but you'll need to know how to recognize a good fabric and the perfect cut: one that won't pull tight at the crotch, make folds on your leg, form horizontal zebra stripes, assume a marbled aspect, get pulled thin over your thighs and calves, be too shiny, pill, or run at the touch of a fingernail. The gold medalists (Miss Helen, Dim, Gerbe) all have their best-sellers, especially in the heavier deniers and more opaque meshes.

It goes without saying that we are partial to makers who are exacting about their knits and dyeing techniques (Wolford and FALKE Luxury Line). Their pantyhose are as comfortable as a second skin, the mesh is even throughout, and the seams are discreet. They improve the appearance of the leg and they last a long time.

SHEER OR OPAQUE?

The higher the denier, the more opaque the tight. The lower the denier, the sheerer. Here are some tips that can help you select the right denier for a particular outfit or occasion.

➡ **Sheer and transparent pantyhose** (between 5 and 20 deniers) is the most fragile. The slightest snag can cause a run or ladder.

In flesh tones, an ultra-sheer or sheer pantyhose will dress up a woman who can't go barelegged. Choose a color that is close to your skin tone and not too shiny. Too light has an old-fashioned look. Too dark and you look as if you fell asleep in the tanning booth.

In black, a very sheer pantyhose can accompany sophisticated outfits (a suit, an evening dress) or an outrageously sexy one (a sheath dress with high-heeled sandals). Period. Avoid wearing it with blue-jean shorts (= overgrown teen) or with a wool dress, down jacket, and pointy boots (= old before her time).

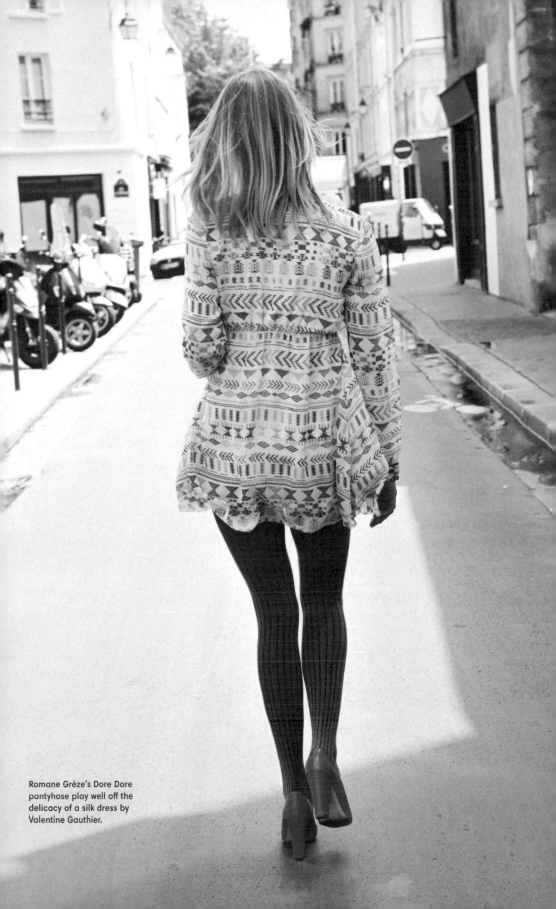

Romane Grèze's Dore Dore pantyhose play well off the delicacy of a silk dress by Valentine Gauthier.

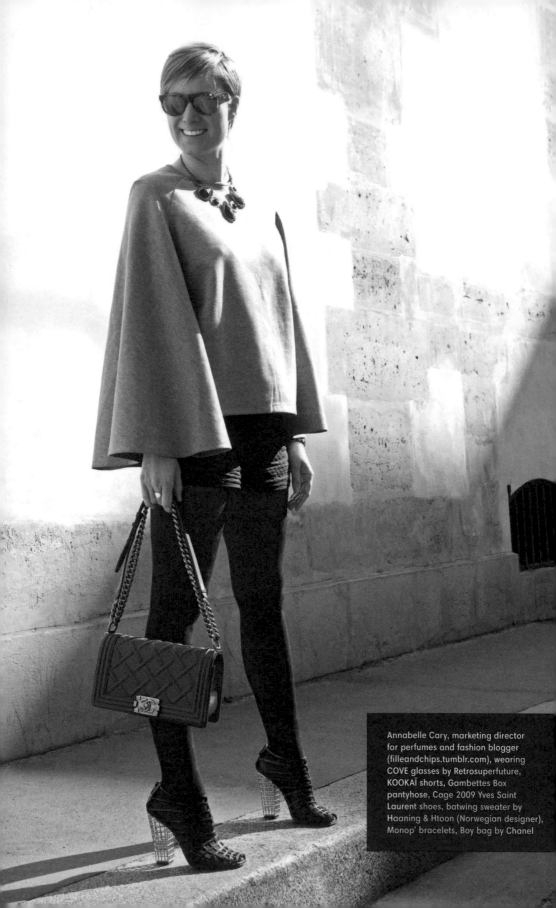

Annabelle Cary, marketing director for perfumes and fashion blogger (filleandchips.tumblr.com), wearing COVE glasses by Retrosuperfuture, KOOKAÏ shorts, Gambettes Box pantyhose, Cage 2009 Yves Saint Laurent shoes, batwing sweater by Haaning & Htoon (Norwegian designer), Monop' bracelets, Boy bag by Chanel

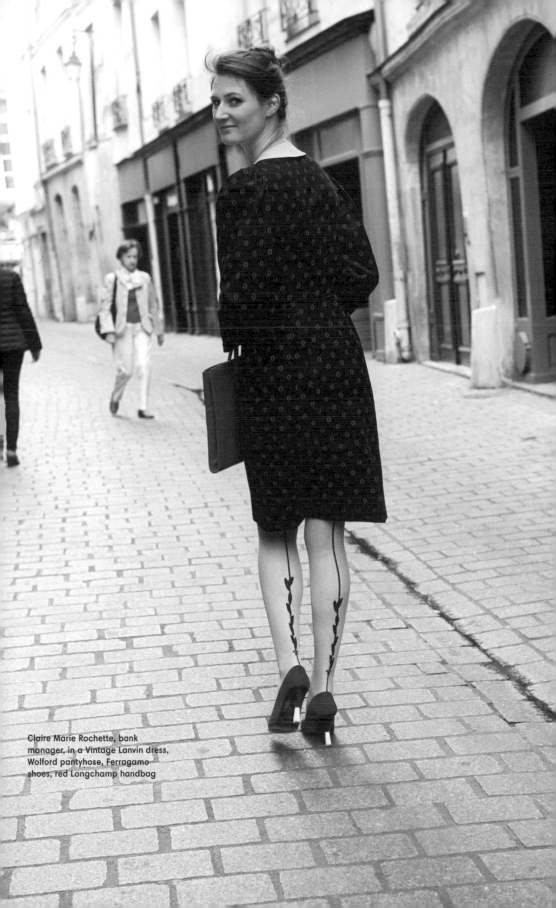

Claire Marie Rochette, bank
manager, in a Vintage Lanvin dress,
Wolford pantyhose, Ferragamo
shoes, red Longchamp handbag

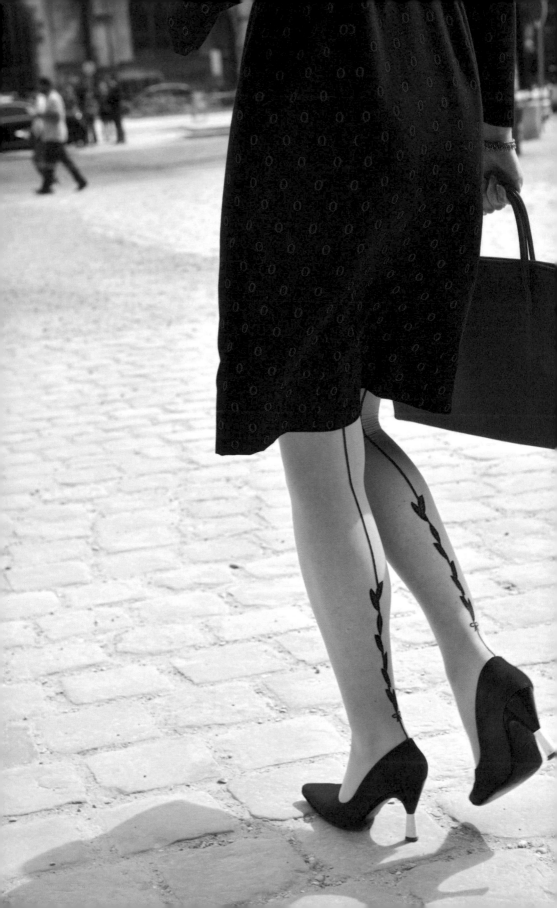

"I wear skirts and shorts a lot, and I collect fun pantyhose to personalize my outfits. I like opaque tights with openwork motifs (diamonds, etc.), but also colors, especially fuchsia."

Annabelle Cary, marketing director for perfumes and fashion blogger (filleandchips.tumblr.com)

. . . .

➡ **Semi-opaque** (between 25 and 40 deniers) **and opaque** (between 50 and 100 deniers) are the easiest to handle. They go with everything and last longer.

When it comes to more opaque tights, forget about light tones that will date you and make your legs look thicker. Stick to black or a vivid color, which leaves plenty of choices! Also, look to the quality of the mesh, and no sparkles—unless you're trying for the granny look.

Opaque tights allow you to wear short skirts, above-the-knee dresses, and shorts—even when you're older than twenty-five. They can be matched with thicker fabrics (tweed, wools…) as well as with lighter ones (silk, cotton, muslin…).

However, it's best to avoid very opaque tights if you have heavy legs and joints. In these cases, consider elasticized tights (spandex or elastane) that sculpt the leg and sometimes also the thigh and stomach.

. . . .

Are Socks with Designs on Them OK?

Yes, but avoid crude prints (square flower petals) and dorky drawings (pink elephants). You can go to town on polka dots, stripes, plaids, leopard prints, zebra prints, python…

. . . .

AND THEN THERE ARE SOCKS

We may as well say it: We steer clear of transparent mid-calf socks, especially in skin tones. Definitely a turn-off. Argh! It's impossible not to think of that horrible band that cuts into your calf!

Today, even support socks can be found in black. So, yes to nylon socks, but they should be opaque, either black or lace. And a big yes to "real" socks—the ones that are made of cotton, mercerized cotton yarn, or wool. And it's OK if we see them between the bottom of your cropped trouser or rolled-up chinos and your shoes. They'll bring a welcome touch of color. You can also slip them into a pair of open sandals or pumps: Not everyone likes that style, but it's been a favorite of ours for years!

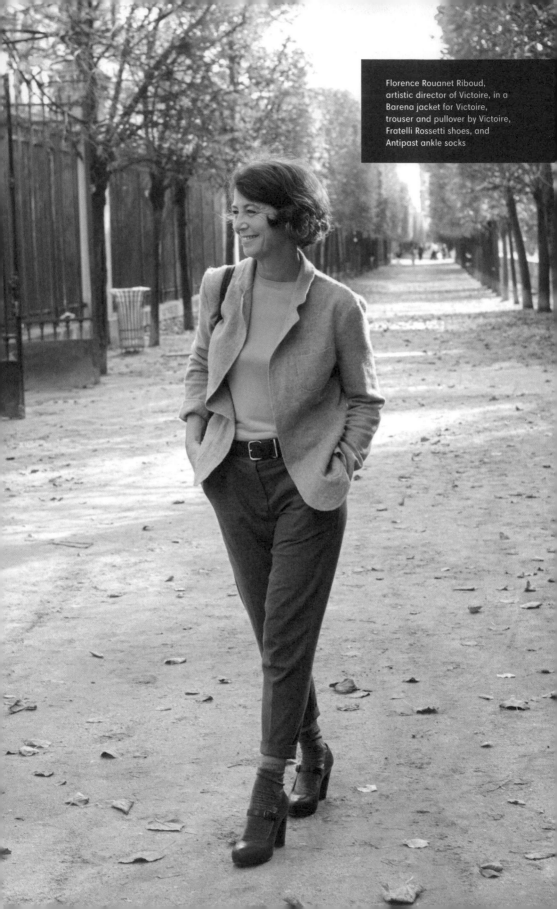

Florence Rouanet Riboud, artistic director of Victoire, in a Barena jacket for Victoire, trouser and pullover by Victoire, Fratelli Rossetti shoes, and Antipast ankle socks

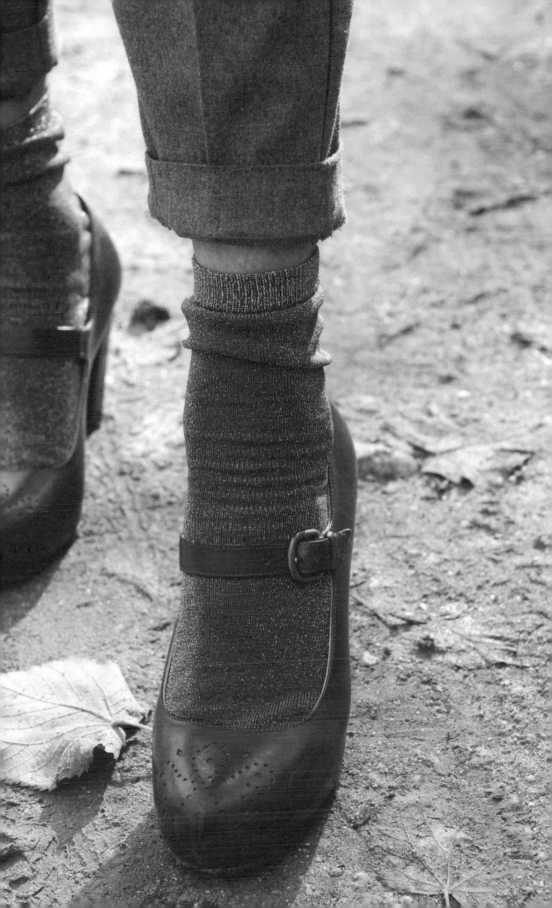

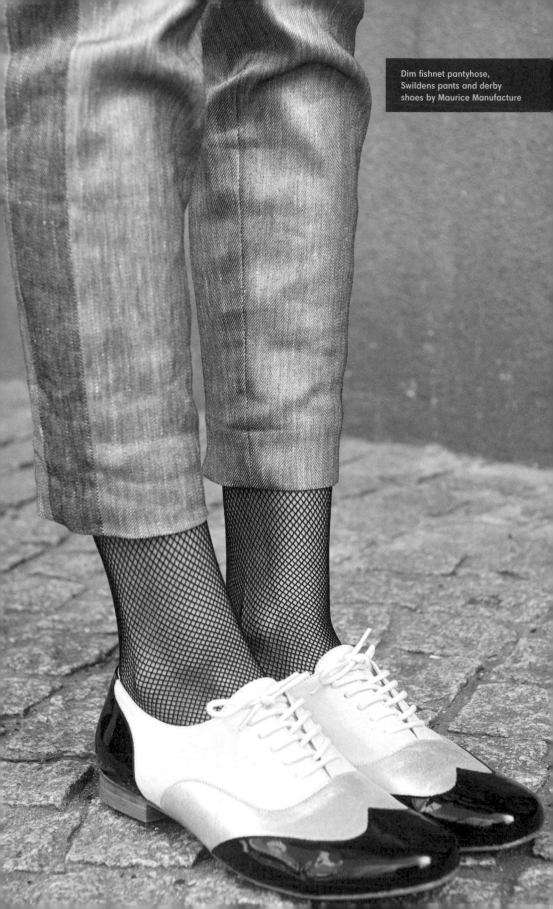

Dim fishnet pantyhose, Swildens pants and derby shoes by Maurice Manufacture

WANT A LITTLE FANTASY?

FISHNETS

NO. We don't need to tell you that it's better to stay away from fishnet stockings altogether than to wear them hooker-style with red patent leather stilettos and a leatherette miniskirt. Stay away from grunge styling as well. No pairing fishnets with a plaid shirt, shorts, and combat boots.

Yes. Fishnets can give you a neo-pinup look when worn with a below-the-knee pencil skirt and motorcycle boots, oxfords, or couture pumps.

POLKA DOTS

NO. With a classic skirt and high-cut pumps, you're returning to the 1980s. That's fun if you're twenty years old. But if you're older, it will make you look sixty-five, even if you're only thirty-five!

Yes. Wear them with a glamorous outfit. At a formal party, for instance, with a structured dress and high-heeled Jimmy Choos.

LACE

NO. The ones with the false garter-belts or drawn-on tattoos… they're just in bad taste.

Yes. Pick a true lace pattern, or else stay away from them! The openwork effect gives a lighter look to your leg and lessens the "massiveness" of opaque tights. Lace pantyhose looks good on everyone and can pep up a slightly too classic dress. But it has to be worn with a sober outfit; we don't want to see lace and frilliness together. Lace goes well with more masculine shoes (loafers or oxfords with high or low heels).

COLOR

NO. Avoid certain loud color combinations entirely, such as red + black (Cruella de Vil), red + green (Santa's elf), and colors that are too flashy.

Yes. Pantyhose in orange, plum, peacock blue, or raspberry are perfect to boost a low-key outfit in brown, gray, khaki, or taupe. Also consider trying dark blue or charcoal tights, which are softer than black and perfect with dark brown or red shoes. If you're feeling bold, try fuchsia.

DESIGNS AND PATTERNS

NO. Small flowers and diamonds look cute on a little girl. On adults they just look pathetic.

Yes. Leopard and reptile prints are worth trying if they're on the subtle side, but only with chic clothes and elegant shoes. Example: knee-length dress and high-heeled booties.

WOOL

NO. Forget 100-percent acrylic pantyhose that will pill in a few hours and make everything else you are wearing look crummy. Bet on 100-percent cotton or wool.

Yes. With wide ribs or cables, woolen tights can set off a slightly retro muslin dress or even a silk skirt. Add shoes with wooden soles or work boots, and you have a very fetching winter look.

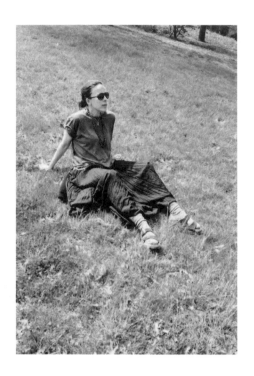

Some of our favorite sock brands

Happy Socks

Tabio

Archiduchesse

Badelaine

Here are some easy-to-follow rules for those who are unsure how to proceed:

➡ If you're afraid of making a mistake, match your socks to the color of your shoes: black + black, dark brown + dark brown, gray + gray… You can also experiment with Lurex socks for a little fun.

➡ If you wear dark shoes, then stick to dark socks (no ankle-length white socks à la Michael Jackson). If you choose burgundy, dark gray, peacock blue, dark brown, or gray, you can hardly go wrong.

➡ If your shoes are a bright color, then select socks that match a color in your outfit or play with subtle contrasts.

"My guy thinks wearing socks with Birkenstocks is the least sexy thing in the world… but I just find it so cute!"

Juliette Swildens on her Facebook page

HAPPY PAIRINGS

➪ Black shoes + pale-gray, peacock-blue, plum, or dark-green socks

➪ Red shoes + beige or pale-pink socks

➪ Navy shoes + dark-gray, dark-green, or raspberry socks

➪ Gray shoes + sky-blue, orangish, or forest-green socks

➪ Dark-brown shoes + mustard, red, or orange socks

➪ Metallic gold shoes + beige or khaki socks

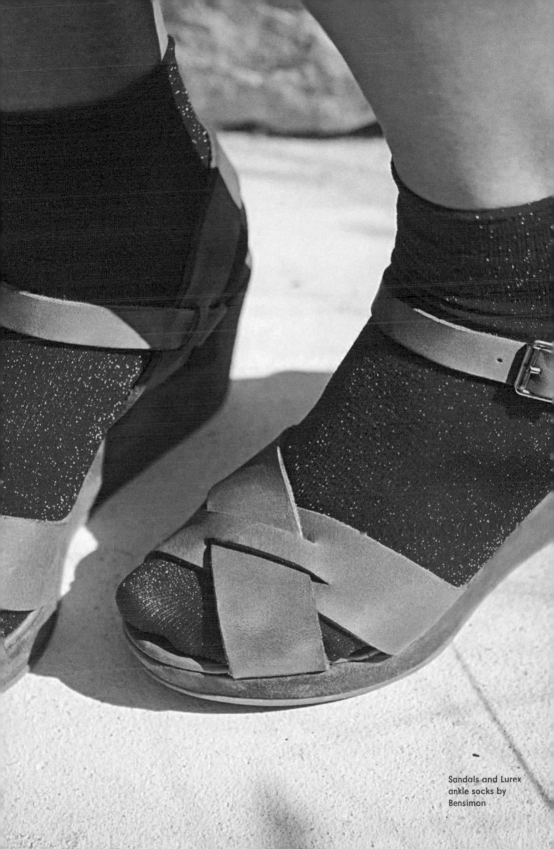

Sandals and Lurex
ankle socks by
Bensimon

Sandra Choi

CREATIVE DIRECTOR OF JIMMY CHOO

· · · · · · · · · · · · · · · · ·

"I remember the shoes that I wore on important occasions, like the night that I met my husband. They tell a story, and I'm forever attached to them."

What do you notice first in a woman?

I'd be lying if I didn't say that I noticed a woman's feet first, but it's because of my work, a kind of occupational hazard.

Why are women so obsessed with shoes?

Women always have a privileged relationship with shoes. It begins very early, when little girls read stories about magical shoes, like in *The Wizard of Oz*. The transformative power of a pair of shoes is implanted at a tender age, the capacity of the woman wearing them to enter literally and figuratively into the skin of a character: A powerful woman in black stiletto heels, a glamorous siren in strappy silver sandals, or a cool rebel in motorcycle boots. Shoes are a constant in our wardrobes—they can instantly perk up an outfit. So spending a little more for luxury high heels is a good investment because you don't get tired of them!

Is it possible to be sexy in flats?

What's sexy is self-confidence, the fact of being slightly reserved, a touch mystery. You can wear spike-heeled thigh-highs or androgynous flats and still be sexy, but you always have to stay on the right side of sexy. It's all in your attitude and your way of carrying yourself.

What do you think of Parisian women and French women generally? Are they still a source of inspiration?

There are women all over the world who inspire me, but more in France. French women have an innate sense of style. Whether it's their way of speaking or their effortless seductiveness, they are really sexy! When I start to work on a new collection, I like to imagine who the Jimmy Choo woman is, walking around in the streets. I like to start off by thinking of her as a beautiful Parisian woman.

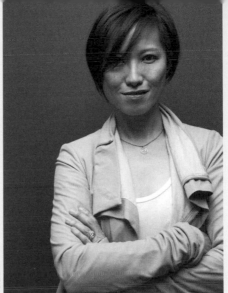

Is there anything about shoes that you don't like?

I don't like to see women who aren't comfortable in their shoes. When shoes look uncomfortable or the wrong size, it's not pretty and it's really too bad.

Do you remember the first shoe you ever designed?

It was in 1992. Obviously they weren't as sexy as today's. Especially because at that time I wasn't a professional!

What are your criteria for a well-designed and well-built shoe?

I first need an idea or a dream, something that gets my attention and prompts me to create. Then you have to scrupulously respect the fundamentals of shoe design—the cut, the last, the height of the heels, the construction process. Every millimeter counts! If you're working with straps and lacing, how wide should they be and where should they come in contact with the foot? How do they work? How are they worn? All these factors have to be taken into account, and if all these criteria aren't respected, it's a waste of time.

Must one suffer to be beautiful?

Ideally, I'd like everything to be comfortable, but if a few extra centimeters make the shoe really incredible, you'll feel magnificent and the pain will be quickly forgotten!

As a woman, do you design differently than a man? What is your first priority when you design for women?

I don't know if there's a difference... I've always been a woman! I agree that being able to wear the shoes that you create is an advantage. You can draw everything on paper, but as a designer the fact of touching and wearing your creation makes you understand better how to improve it. I'm also aware that my idea of perfection might not be the same as yours. So it's very important to try the shoes on a model and to look at them objectively. Shoes are a functional art. If you can't wear them, they're only artwork!

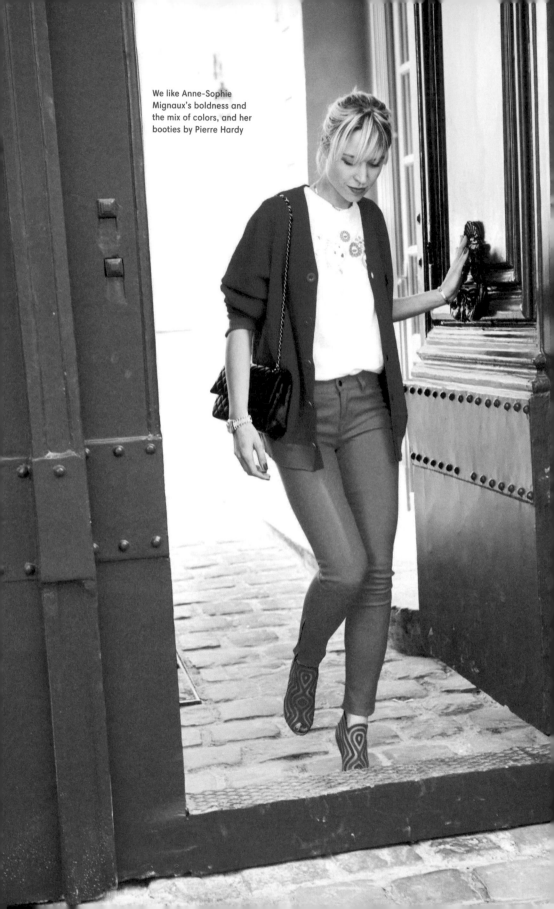

We like Anne-Sophie Mignaux's boldness and the mix of colors, and her booties by Pierre Hardy

INDISPUTABLE, IRREFUTABLE
FASHION FAUX PAS

. . . .

Fashion is subjective: You start to find something charming while other people identify it as a notorious fashion faux pas. Socks with sandals? Horrors! But a daring fashion statement is not always a faux pas!

You're allowed to hate Lurex socks with oxfords, find Swedish clogs unsexy, or swear by snow boots. These are all questions of taste.

The real transgressions against taste are the ones that everybody agrees to. Some will earn you only a light reprimand from the fashion police, while others will cost you a lot of points on your fashion license.

ERRORS OF INATTENTION

➡ **Leaving the sticker on the sole of your shoe. Oh really, is it visible?**

When you're sitting with your legs crossed, it's all anyone can see. And while you're at it, snip off the tag that's poking out from the end of your scarf!

➡ **The line showing the reinforced toe of your sock when wearing open-toed shoes.**

The rule is simple: Avoid acrylic mid-calf stockings and choose cotton or wool instead.

➡ **Cracked heels and badly trimmed toenails. Why not chipped nail polish?**

We won't even mention the lone, wiry hair sticking up from your big toe!

➡ **Worn, unpolished shoes.**

Make a distinction between shoes that show a patina of use and cheap shoes that age badly. Abraded heels, scratched leather, tired soles… toss them in the garbage!

➡ **Pointy shoes with the toe sticking up.**

There is pointed and then there's *pointed*. A pretty little snout is one thing, but a big old beak that seems to want to bite you is another.

➡ **Low-rent animal prints.**

If you're as much a fan of leopard, snake, and zebra prints as we are, be very exacting about the quality of the animal imitation. One blogger talks about finding "leoperfects."

➡ **Bad knockoffs of "it" shoes.**

Naturally not everyone can afford (or is willing) to buy themselves a pair of Dickers by Isabel Marant, Susan by Chloé, Pirate Boots by Vivienne Westwood, the Sélina by Bottes Gardiane, or Tropéziennes by Rondini... to name a few. Lovely knockoffs exist, but you have to be very careful about the details: No cheap substitutes, please. Your whole look will suffer as a result. And your wallet, too, when it transpires that your fake St. Tropez sandals won't even last the summer.

FAILURES OF INSPIRATION

➡ **Just make it black.**

Of course, black is a good option for your wardrobe. But you should avoid it when it's just the easy solution, along the lines of "I really don't have the time to figure out if this suits me." And anyway, black doesn't actually go with everything. Natural leather, burgundy, and dark gray are sometimes "easier." Also, if it's an inexpensive leather item, it can sometimes look terrible in black.

➡ **Copying and pasting trends.**

Just because motorcycle boots have become classics or pool slides are the latest must-have, it doesn't necessarily mean that you need to own a pair. Look for shapes that suit you and will fit in well with your wardrobe.

THE WRONG HEM LENGTH...

➡ **A long pant paired with flat soles: It makes you look shorter.**

With ballerinas or very flat oxfords, choose either a trouser cropped at the ankle or a dress.

➡ **A trouser that is too short at the hem: disgraceful.**

When you have trousers hemmed, you have to decide on the height of the heels you plan to wear them with. You can always roll up the narrow leg of your chinos and jeans, or bunch up a pair of slim jeans, but you can't change the height of a wider trouser leg, which is meant to almost engulf the shoe and not stare down at it from above.

➡ **The classic straight-cut, mid-thigh skirt with knee-high boots: old-fashioned.**

To make your figure look lighter, you need to show more leg: opt for ankle boots instead.

➡ **A mid-length skirt with pumps: too grandmotherly.**

The mid-calf length is a problem anyway. It looks good only with boots, a pair of 1970s-style T-strap sandals, or men's oxfords.

THE WRONG PANTYHOSE

➡ **Ultra-sheer pantyhose with boots.**

These are two cultures in opposition. You must choose sides, period.

➡ **Sheer pantyhose in a pale shade with dark shoes.**

Why not just combine these items with a flowered muumuu?

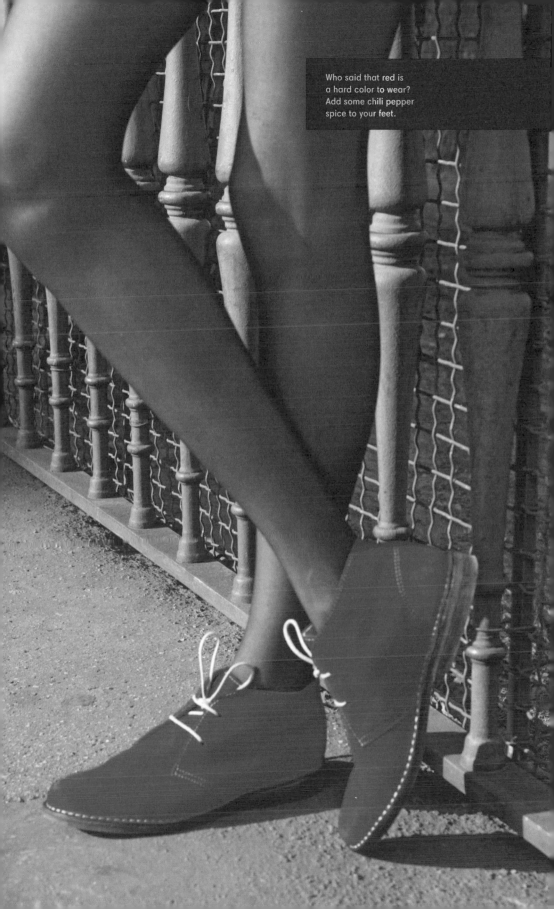

Who said that **red** is
a hard color **to wear**?
Add some **chili pepper**
spice to **your feet**.

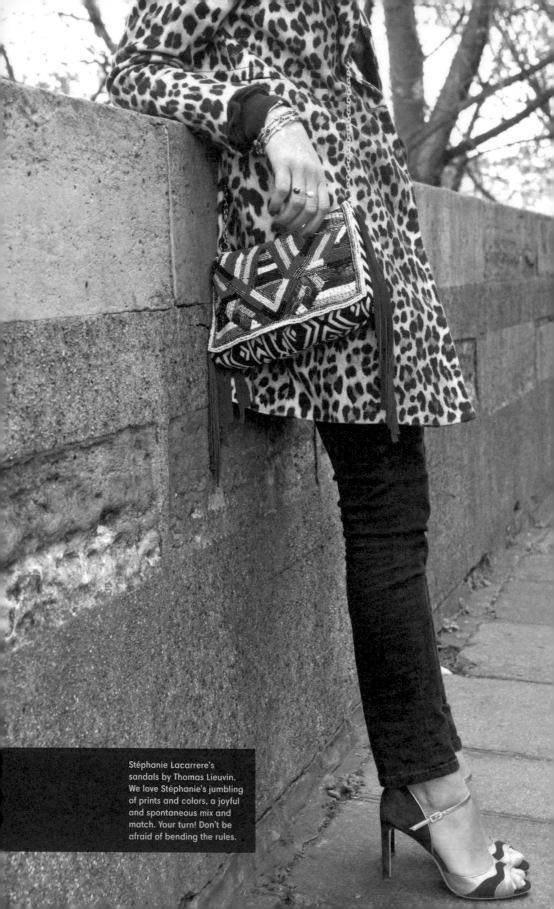

Stéphanie Lacarrere's sandals by Thomas Lieuvin. We love Stéphanie's jumbling of prints and colors, a joyful and spontaneous mix and match. Your turn! Don't be afraid of bending the rules.

➡ **Dark brown tights with black boots.**

Next to this desperately sad pairing, *Romeo and Juliet* is a hilarious comedy.

ERRORS IN SIZE

➡ **Toes that are tensed.**

Too small? Too high? Too big? Too slippery? Your toes always tense up when your shoes are the wrong size. With sandals, it's plainly visible. With closed shoes, a person can tell from your tense facial expression. No, your shoes won't grow a size bigger. No, your foot will not "adapt." Yes, you have to be comfortable from the moment you try the shoes on.

➡ **The heel height is wrong.**

It's not just a question of the shoe's shape but of how you carry yourself. The same applies to the shoe's style: Shoes that look great on everyone just don't exist. You have to find "your" style of pump, boot, ankle boot… Yes, it takes work. But once you have put in the time, you won't make any more mistakes.

➡ **The height doesn't flatter your leg.**

When you choose shoes, you don't want to look just at your feet but at your whole figure. Take your shape into account, the size of your joints (ankles that swell?), the slimness or roundness of your calves, your knees, your lower thighs…

➡ **Zippered boots that flare at the top make the leg seem to float.**

A classic boot should marry the leg. If you want boots that pay no attention to the slenderness of your leg, choose a cowboy boot or a Camarguaise roper.

➡ **Knee-high boots that constrain the fat around your knees.**

If you have chubby calves, choose a low boot and control pantyhose. Or booties.

➡ **Straps that turn your swollen toes into overcooked mini-sausages.**

If swelling is an issue, stay away from narrow straps and choose wider ones that don't pass between the toes.

➡ **Heels that don't work with your figure.**

If you're small and round, drop any notion of walking on stilts. Stick with heel heights that are in proportion to your body type.

➡ **Walking like a stork in a minefield.**

Practice walking in heels before you appear in public. The mission may not be as impossible as you think. But if you continue to wobble, then you might want to give up on the Victoria Beckham six-inch heels. You'll still look great in heels that are "only" three inches.

Inès de la Fressange

AMBASSADOR FOR THE MAISON ROGER VIVIER

. . . .

"Shoes, like perfume, don't allow for mediocrity."

How many pairs of shoes do you have in your closet?

Love knows no bounds! All the same, there must be about a hundred, counting sneakers, espadrilles, sandals. But I weed them out often, and I try not to keep the ones I don't wear.

Do you keep your favorites for a long time, or are you good at throwing [shoes] away?

I don't keep them, because women's shoes are often a lot less pretty when they get worn. On the other hand, leather oxfords that can be polished, as long as you keep shoe trees in them, can be kept a long time. I try to have wooden shoe trees for this kind of shoe. For all the others, I have plastic ones I bought at Ikea, because not only does it keep your shoes in better shape but it also looks more orderly in your closet.

Do you dress according to the shoes you're going to wear or vice versa?

If I have a new pair, I'll do anything possible to find an outfit that goes with them, of course! Normally, though, I'll pay attention to the weather. Your choice of shoes can totally affect your general look: A pair of white jeans with sandals, stilettos, or motorcycle boots—those are three entirely different silhouettes. It's even more important with evening outfits, where flats can give you a much more contemporary look (though I know the idea is a nightmare to many women!). One day, a friend suggested that I wear very dressy, jeweled ballerina flats to spend the day in. The idea at first struck me as surrealistic, but in the end as excellent!

How many shoes does a woman need to be well-supplied?

Fewer than you have in your closet...but of better quality! Shoes, like perfume, don't allow for mediocrity. It's completely different from clothes: You can dress well anywhere on a small budget. With shoes, it's more complicated. You could imagine a list:

A pair of pumps (black, let's say); a pair of ballerinas; a pair of boots; a pair of Converse sneakers; a pair of sandals; a pair of formal, dressy evening shoes. But let's be clear that when it comes to feet, reason has no say!

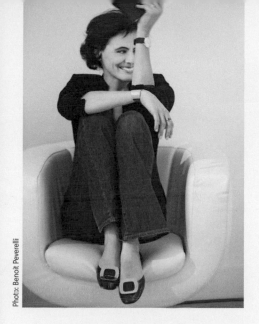

What shoes are absolutely necessary, according to you?

With a pair of black ballerinas, you can do anything. But some women would prefer to leave their husbands, turn their dog into a doormat, and do without a washing machine rather than wear flats.

What accounts for a shoe's elegance?

Personally, I don't like shoes that have a visible welt around the edge. There's a certain visible craftsmanship in the proportions and the choice of materials that you start to recognize after long exposure to quality—ridges on the front, for example, that only luxury models have. Professionals, I believe, can quickly determine the quality of a shoe. It's a little like eighteenth-century furniture; it jumps out.

Fortunately, there are shoes that aren't prohibitive that can all the same be very elegant: Rondini sandals, for example. But "elegance" no longer seems to be the clients' primary criterion. I'm nostalgic for the Mancinis, Perugias, Blahniks of the early days, where extravagance combined effortlessly with elegance. It's one of the reasons I work for Roger Vivier, which is a company that has kept this ethos.

Is there a style of shoe to avoid?

Anything I might name could be taken by a talented designer and brilliantly interpreted. If I were to say, for instance, a cowboy boot with a white fringe and rhinestones, it could be disgusting or… irresistible! Fashion teaches us to adore what we started off detesting.

Are there faux pas that are unforgivable?

I work at a company where one shoe style is particularly copied [by other manufacturers]: The one with a buckle, worn most visibly by Catherine Deneuve in *Belle de Jour*. None of the knockoffs come at all close to the original. If a person is not able to see the difference between the original and the fake, to understand that this difference is everything, then yes, that's unpardonable. If you don't have the money to buy yourself the original, it's better to get another, completely different shoe.

"I don't know who invented high heels, but all women owe him a lot." Do you agree with Marilyn Monroe, or do you believe that high heels and seductiveness are not necessarily related?

Think of the photographs of Marilyn that have impressed you the most. The one with her Irish sweater? Or naked on a bed? Or dancing? Talking? Staring? Smiling? Or with windswept hair? In any case, it wasn't her feet that you noticed. If certain women feel better in heels, they are seductive because they feel beautiful, not because they are four inches taller. The movement is sensual, not the height. When Ava Gardner dances, she's barefoot, and what we like about Marilyn is her soul, not her heels.

A woman who wears heels and is taller than her husband or companion—has that entered the mainstream?

Yes, ma'am! And she can even be a few years older and have a few more euros in the bank. Crazy, no?

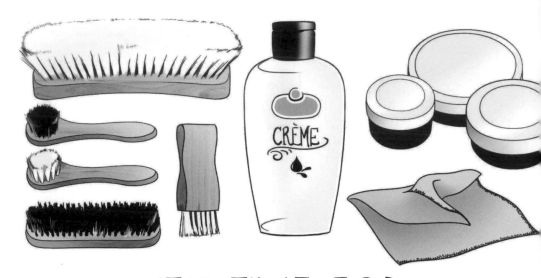

IT'S TIME FOR
A SHINE
AND A GOOD SPRING CLEAN

Before buffing our leather goods to a high shine, we need to screw up our courage and toss out the clunkers and the clodhoppers in our collection, and create a real showcase for our shoes. Those ratty old ones hiding under beds and dressers or skulking in the back of closets... out they go!

INTO THE GARBAGE CAN!

Be merciless toward worn-out shoes: ground-down heels, suspect soles, creased toes, scratched leather, frayed straps...

You deserve better than these leftover bits that do nothing for your look. No, you'll never wear them again. All the better.

Go ahead and get rid of the shoes that look old-fashioned. Even if certain styles come back, the old ones will look out of date. Today's pointed toe has nothing in common with the pointed toe of the 1990s. Same for today's wedges, which look nothing like the wedges of the 1970s.

In a word, be wary of yesterday's heels, last decade's toe boxes, and granny-style uppers, as they can instantly add years to your wardrobe.

INTO THE ARCHIVES!

If you're too attached to certain shoes to make them disappear forever, put them away carefully:

- Shine them.
- Stuff them with tissue paper.
- Put them in a cloth bag or wrap them in newspaper.

You can pull them out again in ten years and show them to your daughter, who'll be astonished that anyone ever wore such things!

DIVIDE YOUR SHOES ACCORDING TO SEASON AND OCCASION

On one side, summer styles, and on the other, winter. You can also add a section for shoes that you only wear for specific events (dancing, hiking, going to the beach…). You'll be able to see it all more clearly and have ready access to your everyday shoes, which you can alternate more readily.

Slip the pairs that you're not using during the current season into big transparent boxes or storage bags (you can find them in every department store or furniture outlet) and store them on top of tall dressers or under beds and benches.

GET ORGANIZED

If you're the lucky owner of many pairs of shoes *and* you're a patient woman, you can glue pictures of your shoes onto the storage boxes.

Or put them in a photo album on your phone to scroll through when selecting clothes. We know highly organized women who swear by this system.

If you find that metal or fabric shoe racks that attach to a door don't work for you, or if your shoe closet is too small, find a piece of furniture that you can use in lieu of a rack. Examples: an industrial steel cabinet, an old-fashioned garden shelf, an open Ikea bookcase on which you can keep wicker baskets… You can also place a narrow bookcase in a closet or a hallway and camouflage it with a pretty piece of fabric.

A LITTLE LOVE

A simple secret for keeping your favorite shoes as long as possible: Take good care of them at regular intervals.

Raphaël from the Paris cobbler Pulin, which has a great reputation for resoling shoes in a variety of colors, has helped us separate the wheat from the chaff.

· ·

THE BEST SHOE CREAM

Saphir is a French company. Family-owned, it was founded in 1920 and its products are now sold around the world. It works with and advises all the most prestigious French leather manufacturers and its unchanged recipe (turpentine with animal, vegetable, and mineral waxes) has earned a sterling reputation among lovers of shoes.

Despite conventional wisdom, not every shoe should be fitted with a sole protector. While outer sole guards are a good idea for shoes made of leather or kid, boots, or ankle boots worn every day, it is not necessary for "fragile" shoes worn only in the evening or shoes made of delicate materials such as fabric, lace, or satin… The light, pure line of the shoe must be preserved.

The secret of having good sole protectors is to wear the shoe for two or three days before having the sole guards applied. The leather softens and forms "walking creases."

MY SHOES HAVE GOTTEN WET! WHAT SHOULD I DO?

Never bring them anywhere near a source of heat. A wet shoe should be kept far from the radiator and the fireplace!

Instead, stuff them full of tissue paper or newspaper and place them on their sides for twenty-four hours to dry completely. When they are dry, you can put a wooden shoe tree inside and begin hydrating the leather.

SHOE CREAM, NOT POLISH

For women's shoes, whose leather stays very pigmented compared to men's, use a cream rather than a polish. The best shoe cream available is from Saphir, a Paris-based shoe cream company that offers ninety-five different shades. They're bound to have the color you need. The creams contain natural beeswax, carnauba wax, and almond oil, which will rehydrate and nourish the leather. The creams do not contain silicone, which is the enemy of all hides. The treatment will soften and renew your favorite pumps.

Polish, which is thicker, is most often used for men's shoes and gives them a hard shine.

"Leather, like human skin, needs hydration and gentle treatment, but you have to use the right products," says Marc Moura, CEO of Saphir. "Using NIVEA or other moistening lotions is a myth, even if certain heavier leathers absorb it. You need to use products adapted to the tanning process that leather has undergone."

"Don't go near those ready-to-use sponge polishers that they sell in department stores. They are full of silicone and will ruin your shoes!" says Raphaël, of the Pulin cobbler shop. "They look great the first time you use them because the silicone shines up like a mirror, but that plasticized layer will keep the leather from breathing and make it crack—and there's no way to repair that," says Marc Moura.

For a high luster, buff the leather with a stocking, some silk, or a "buffing mitt."

If your pumps are scratched, scuffed, and discolored, use Saphir's renovating cream (a concentrated source of color), which will restore and renew the leather's pigmentation. After it dries, simply apply shoe cream and buff them to a shine. Your handbags and your children's shoes might also benefit from this miracle treatment.

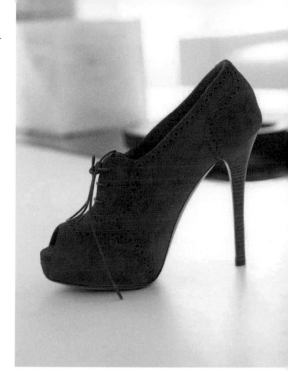

A beautiful shoe from Ralph Lauren must be looked after with the greatest care.

WHAT ABOUT MY SUEDE BOOTS?

Raphaël, from the Pulin cobbler shop, advises waterproofing suede, as it will offer some protection. Once again, you should invest in quality products and stay away from any that contain silicone or other "miracle" resins.

Suede is like a fabric: It can be washed, but again you need to use the right products. Saphir has developed a special soap for this task called Omnidaim. It contains gentle solvents that form a lather and should be applied with a silk brush over the entire surface of the shoe. It washes away dirt and refreshes nubuck's natural color. It is more complicated to use than a spray, but it's often the only solution. For small spots, a suede brush that erases the stain and raises the nap is enough, but it takes a certain degree of skill not to blemish or wear away the suede.

As for aerosols that revive color, be sure to read the labels and find an eco-friendly product.

Now it's up to you…

SHOE CARE ON THE WEB

Here are the sites to visit to learn everything you need to know about beauty products for shoes. Click on the British flag for English text:

www.valmour.com

www.avel.com

A SHORT NOTE ABOUT LABELS

. . . .

*Read labels carefully. They provide information on the
uppers, the lining, the insole, and the outer sole.*

Learn your shoe vocabulary so that you know which part of the shoe is which:

➡ **The upper:** The external surface attached to the outer sole.

➡ **The lining and the insole taken together:** The inside of the shoe.

➡ **The outer sole:** The bottom of the shoe, subject to wear from walking and attached to the upper.

The label must also indicate the primary materials composing the shoe. A major component is a material that represents at least 80 percent of a particular part of the shoe (upper, lining and insole, or outer sole).

If no material is a major component, then the two main materials constituting the shoe must be listed.

"Leather" designates the hide of an animal, its fibrous structure more or less intact after tanning. Naming the animal species from which the hide comes is not obligatory.

"Full-grain leather" designates a hide that retains its original grain as present when taken from the animal and from which no layers have been removed by buffing, sanding, or splitting.

"Coated leather" is a product whose coating does not exceed one-third the thickness of the total product but is greater than .15 millimeters.

. . . .

"In France, craftsmanship is not valued, making shoes is an unskilled and despised trade. The financial people destroyed the shoe business, they wanted double-digit returns, but you can't make huge amounts of money off shoes. You have to put in the time to adjust the prototypes, a lot of pieces need to fall into place. Just the heel can cost from 2 to 35 euros, depending on the quality and complexity."
Nathalie Elharrar, creator of the LaRare line

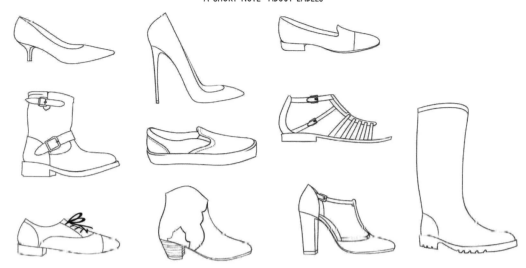

From left to right, top to bottom: kitten heel, stiletto, slipper, motorcycle boot,
slip-on sneaker, Greek sandal, oxford, bootie, T-strap heel, rain boot

· ·

THE SYMBOLS
ON THE BOTTOM OF THE SHOE

In 1996, Europe passed a law requiring shoemakers to label their products.
The label must give the characteristics of the shoe.

 This symbol designates the material as leather.

 This symbol means that the material is coated leather. It is generally seen on linings and has a smooth appearance.

 This symbol designates the material as a textile.

 This symbol designates the material as other than the above.

There are also other symbols that designate specific parts of the shoe:

 This symbol indicates the shoe's upper.

 This symbol indicates the outer sole of the shoe.

 This symbol indicates the inside of the shoe, including the lining and the insole.

OUR FAVORITE ADDRESSES IN PARIS*

*Because we live in Paris, and it's the city we know best.

You can lose your head in the Ali Baba's cave of shoe departments at the Galeries Lafayette or Printemps on Boulevard Haussmann. Or maybe you prefer the selection to be found in little boutiques. We like both!

58m

58, rue Montmartre, 75002 Paris
Girl, don't venture unprepared into this den for shoe collectors or you'll be lost! Acne, Sigerson Morrison, Jérôme Dreyfuss, Véronique Branquinho . . . the happening designs are all here.

ANN TUIL

63, rue de Passy, 75016 Paris
A somewhat safe but relevant selection of contemporary trends. From Sergio Rossi to K. Jacques.

CENTRE COMMERCIAL

2, rue de Marseille, 75010 Paris
The pretty changing room is not the only draw—there is also the selection of tasteful shoes: La Botte Gardiane, Church's, Repetto, and a wide range of Veja sneakers that are respectful to fashion and the environment.

COLETTE

213, rue Saint-Honoré, 75001 Paris
Here you can feast on the offerings of the masters— Alaïa, Givenchy, Giuseppe Zanotti, Alexander Wang— and swoon over those of the younger set: Tabitha Simmons, Sophia Webster, Adieu Paris . . .

FRENCH TROTTERS

128, rue Vieille-du-Temple, 75003 Paris
30, rue de Charonne, 75011 Paris
Worth visiting as much for the easy, chic fashion as for the pretty household linens and flawless selection of shoes by Michel Vivien, Chie Mihara, A.P.C., Avril Gau, and the French Trotters line.

GARRICE

30, rue de Rivoli, 75004 Paris
Freedom and modernity is the credo of this concept store, which has trendy designs and is also the place to find your Fiorentini + Baker motorcycle boots.

IRIS

28, rue de Grenelle, 75007 Paris
This Italian company has made shoes for Marc Jacobs, Chloé, Michael Kors, Jil Sander, and

Claire Marie Rochette in a coat by Adeline André, a necklace accessory by Kobja, and sandals by Yves Saint Laurent

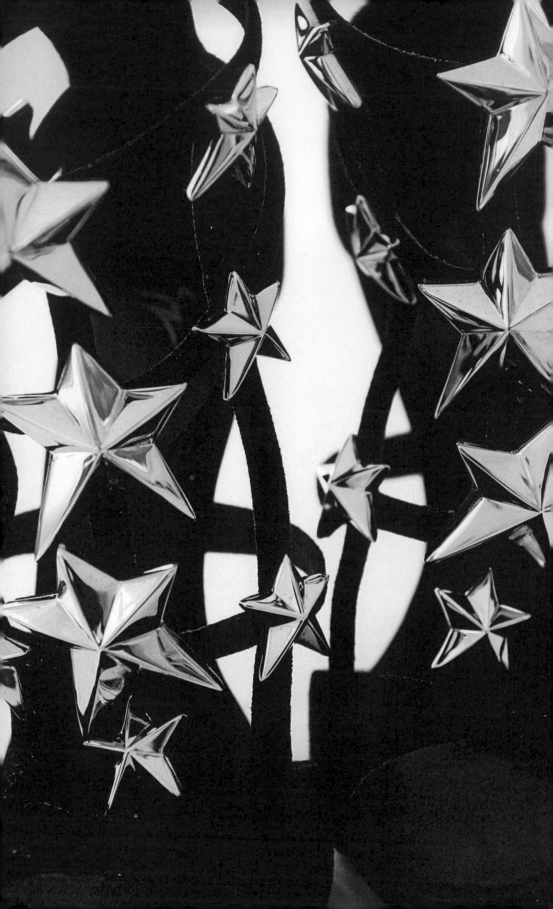

Véronique Branquinho in designs that would make Carrie Bradshaw turn green with envy.

KABUKI

13, rue de Turbigo, 75003 Paris
Started by Barbara Bui in the early 1990s, this mini-boutique devoted to influential shoes is the go-to place of seasoned fashionistas.

LOBATO

6, rue Malher, 75004 Paris
From Pierre Hardy to Proenza Schouler, Michel Vivien, and Ellen Truijen, the shop offers a fine array of the most widely admired designers. It's impossible to make a fashion faux pas here.

MOSS

22, rue de Grenelle, 75007 Paris
If you're looking for discreet ballet flats, look elsewhere. Here, your little feet will blush over the sexy and luxurious offerings.

NOUVELLE AFFAIRE

5, rue Debelleyme, 75003 Paris
An experimental space that is constantly changing according to the interests, whims, and discoveries of the owners. Limited series, small selections, and entire rooms devoted to young designers. Beautiful Carritz sandals can be found here.

DESIGNERS' SHOPS...

ANNABEL WINSHIP

29, rue du Dragon, 75006 Paris
A lovely line boasting glamour, comfort, and good humor; that's the recipe these shoes follow, producing a wow-I've-got-to-have-them effect!

AVRIL GAU

17, rue des Quatre-Vents, 75006 Paris
This brand has avid fans for offering the unusual combination of comfort and glamour.

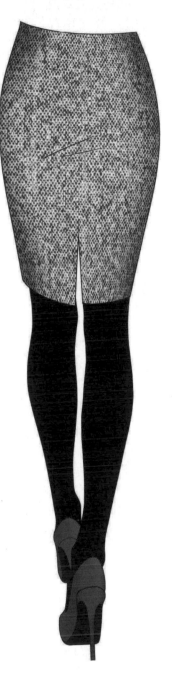

Star-studded Giuseppe Zanotti strappy stilettos

COSMOPARIS

25, rue du Vieux-Colombier, 75006 Paris
97, avenue Victor-Hugo, 75116 Paris
3, rue des Blancs-Manteaux, 75004 Paris

Glamorous, bold, and sexy, this ultra-feminine and inexpensive brand has got Parisian women—and other fashion addicts—rushing to its doors.

C. PETULA

7, rue des Canettes, 75006 Paris

The classics revisited and tweaked with zany and elegant details. Plus quality at a reasonable price.

FERRAGAMO'S CREATIONS

38, rue du Mont-Thabor, 75001 Paris

The store where you find reissues of the mythical shoes created by the Italian brand for stars from Marilyn Monroe to Anna Magnani.

FRED MARZO

11, rue de Thorigny, 75003 Paris (Thursday, Friday, and Saturday from 2 to 7 p.m.)

Vintage styles, reimagined and highly feminine. Quality workmanship using the finest materials. So very chic!

KARINE ARABIAN

4, rue Papillon, 75009 Paris

First known for her shoes with round toes, this designer has gone on to prove that high heels can be both sensual and comfortable.

MELLOW YELLOW

43, rue des Francs-Bourgeois, 75004 Paris

Shoes that are fantastic—in every sense of the term—but don't break your piggybank. Highly wearable impertinence!

PATRICIA BLANCHET

20, rue Beaurepaire, 75010 Paris

Known for its comfortable and inventive ankle boots, this lovely, small brand is set in a wonderful space.

PHILIPPE ZORZETTO

106, rue Vieille-du-Temple, 75003 Paris
257, rue Saint-Honoré, 75001 Paris (by appointment)

Using lasts developed by his grandfather, this shoemaker designs for women as well

"A few years ago, I was looking everywhere for some sturdy brown shoes, but I couldn't find any that I really liked. My mother then got out the ones she'd worn in her youth, and I loved them right away. The idea of walking in my mother's footsteps made it all the better! Since then, she's been stealing them from me again."

Lina Khelfa-Martin wears the never-out-of-fashion ankle boots her mother wore at her age.

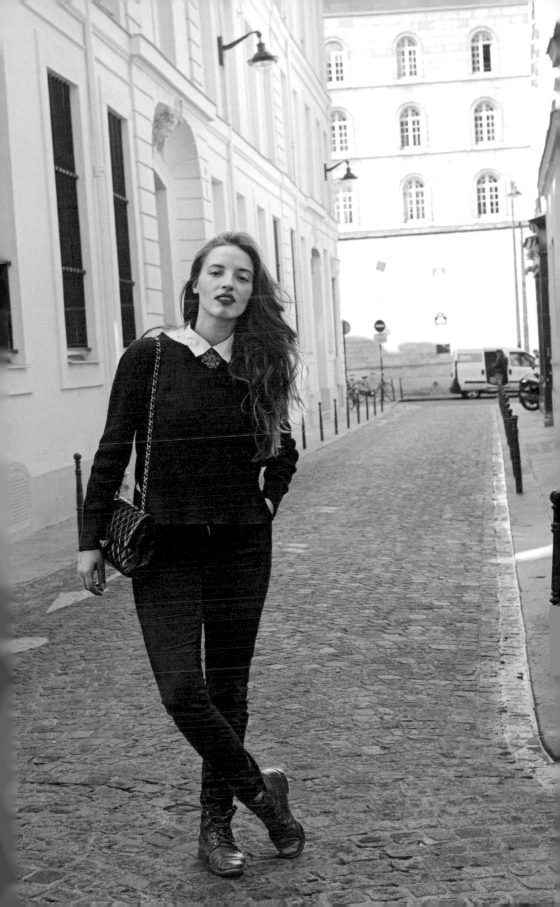

as men. Moccasins, booties, brogues . . . beautiful artisanry, made by hand.

LES PRAIRIES DE PARIS

6, rue du Pré-aux-Clercs, 75007 Paris

23, rue Debelleyme, 75003 Paris

If you love the edgy urban style of designer Laetitia Ivanez's clothes, you will adore her shoes, pumps, booties, and oxfords. Smart and desirable.

RUPERT SANDERSON

5, rue des Petits-Champs, 75001 Paris

These shoes have gained the favor of the stars by their perfect line and their sensuality. You won't be able to resist them!

SURFACE TO AIR

108, rue Vieille-du-Temple, 75003 Paris

This chic Parisian rock brand has a knack for inventing shoes with a crazy design . . . that are still highly wearable. The proof lies in its famous Buckles, often imitated but never equaled, whose successive iterations have been going for seven years and counting.

SWILDENS

18, rue du Vieux-Colombier, 75006 Paris

22, rue de Poitou, 75003 Paris

38, rue Madame, 75006 Paris (also in the 4th and 16th arrondissements)

It's hard not to be convinced by the booties, sandals, and oxfords imagined by Juliette Swildens. Good looks, and easy to live with!

TOSCA BLU

209, rue Saint-Honoré, 75001 Paris

This Milanese brand, which originally specialized in handbags, is now seducing us with its very with-it shoes.

ALSO…

LA BOTTE GARDIANE

25, rue de Charonne, 75011 Paris

CHRISTIAN LOUBOUTIN

19, rue Jean-Jacques-Rousseau, 75001 Paris

DELAGE

15, rue de Valois, 75001 Paris

LA MAISON ERNEST

75, boulevard de Clichy, 75009 Paris

MARIA LUISA

Printemps

64, boulevard Haussmann, 75009 Paris

PIERRE HARDY

Jardins du Palais-Royal, 156, galerie de Valois, 75001 Paris

REPETTO

22, rue de la Paix, 75002 Paris

WALTER STEIGER

83, rue du Faubourg-Saint-Honoré, 75008 Paris

ON THE INTERNET

L'EXCEPTION

www.lexception.com

Here you'll find Annabel Winship, MySuelly, Maurice Manufacture, and many others. Nothing but bold, French brands.

MODE TROTTER

www.modetrotter.com

Heimstone, Bosabo, Philippe Model, Opening Ceremony, Mexicana . . . A very fashion-forward site with a selection that is hip and different, offering looks that are joyous and inspiring.

OFFICE

www.office.co.uk

There's no need for Parisians to cross the Channel to find leopard-print boots and beaded pumps. Everything is here, deliverable as soon as we could want it.

SARENZA

www.sarenza.com

An enormous selection in every style and for every budget, from luxury to bargain with good visuals and comments on the shoes.

SPARTOO

www.spartoo.com

Choices, choices . . . No unpleasant surprises or discoveries. Classic and efficient.

THIS WAY FOR BARGAINS!

JONAK STOCK

44, boulevard de Sébastopol, 75003 Paris

Super prices, depending on the season.

JOURDAN STOCK

23, rue François 1er, 75008 Paris

Yes, it really is a warehouse, perfectly well-ordered and quiet. You can try on shoes here calmly and without pressure.

MELLOW YELLOW STOCK

32, rue de Turbigo, 75003 Paris

If you're easily tempted, it's worth the detour. This small shop is packed year-round with little marked-down treasures by this fun and colorful brand.

PARCOURS STOCK

59, rue Beaubourg, 75003 Paris

A bit of a bazaar, but if you aren't discouraged by the vast stock, you may find what you're looking for—and not just in size eleven-and-a-half.

SABOTINE

35, rue de la Roquette, 75011 Paris

If you overlook this store's uninviting ambience, you may have the good luck to find an item by a premium brand at a bargain price. And that's happiness!

LES SOULIERS.COM

38, rue de Trévise, 75009 Paris

Avril Gau, Pierre Hardy, Michel Vivien, Lanvin, Martin Margiela, Balenciaga, Mon Soulier Paris . . . luxury shoes at up to 60 percent off, and a charming reception by true shoe aficionados.

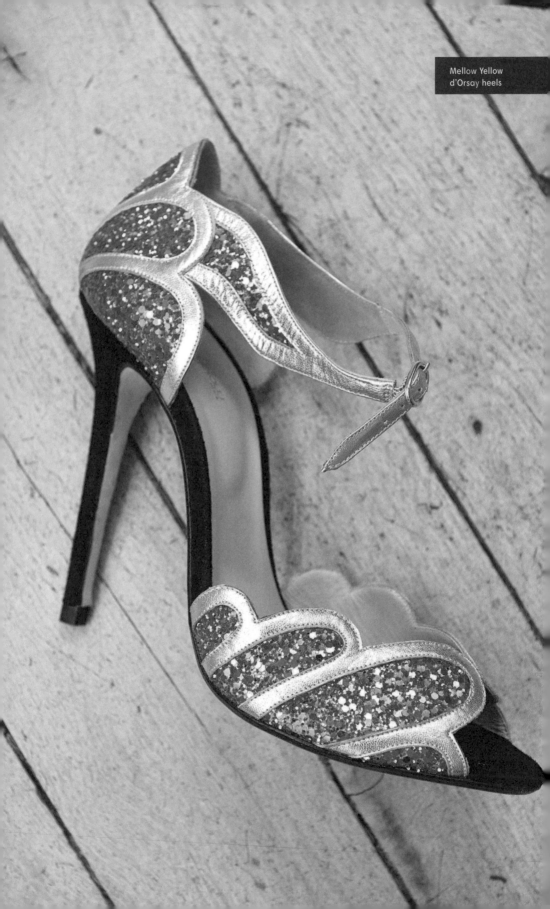

Thanks to Frédérique Poissonnier,
to Miss Glitzy for her wise counsel.

Thanks to Anne de Marnhac,
to François Ravart for his valuable contacts,
to Pierre Carron,
to Mélita Toscan du Plantier.

Thanks to Adeline Roussel,
for her splendid photographs of feet!

Thanks to Nathalie Elharrar for her ginger tea
and her vast knowledge.

Thanks to Anne-Sophie Mignaux
for her contacts and kindness.

Thanks as well to all the beautiful women who love
and collect shoes and who posed for our cameras.

And thanks to the designers who are mad about
Parisian elegance for their magnificent passion.

French-language edition design by Dimitri Maj

ABRAMS IMAGE EDITION

Translated from the French by Willard Wood

Editor: Laura Dozier
Designer: Shawn Dahl, dahlimama inc
Production Manager: Denise LaCongo

Library of Congress Control Number: 2014942739

ISBN: 978-1-4197-1587-7

Printed and bound in Spain
10 9 8 7 6 5 4 3 2 1

Abrams Image books are available at special discounts when purchased in
quantity for premiums and promotions as well as fundraising or educational
use. Special editions can also be created to specification. For details, contact
specialsales@abramsbooks.com or the address below.

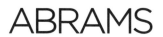

ABRAMS
THE ART OF BOOKS SINCE 1949

115 West 18th Street
New York, NY 10011
www.abramsbooks.com